WHAT ARE MY SPIRITUAL GIFTS?

*How to Discover,
Understand, and Apply
Your Spiritual Gifts*

DR. RYAN DENISON

ALSO FROM DENISON FORUM

The Daily Article email newsletter is news discerned
differently every Monday through Friday.
Subscribe for free at DenisonForum.org.

*A Light Unto My Path:
A Practical Guide to Studying the Bible*

*How to Bless God by Blessing Others:
Words of Wisdom from the Early Church
to Christians Today*

*The Coming Tsunami: Why Christians Are Labeled
Intolerant, Irrelevant, Oppressive, and Dangerous—and
How We Can Turn the Tide*

Biblical Insight to Tough Questions: Vols. 1–10

*Between Compromise and Courage:
The Choice Every Christian Must Make*

*Every Hour I Need Thee:
A Practical Guide to Daily Prayer*

Blessed: Eight Ways Christians Change Culture

*Bright Hope for Tomorrow: How Jesus' Parables
Illuminate Our Darkest Days*

*Respectfully, I Disagree:
How to Be a Civil Person in an Uncivil Time*

Request these books and more at
DenisonForum.org/store

WHAT ARE MY SPIRITUAL GIFTS?

*How to Discover,
Understand, and Apply
Your Spiritual Gifts*

DR. RYAN DENISON

TABLE OF CONTENTS

DO YOU KNOW YOUR SPIRITUAL GIFTS?

If your pastor asked you what your spiritual gifts are, how would you answer?

Do you know for certain how God may have wired you for fulfilling his calling on your life?

Do you know the differences between the spiritual gifts?

And if you have certain spiritual gifts, does that mean you're exempt from the others?

You may have an inkling of how God has gifted you for service to himself, his church, and his world. In fact, you may already be serving in areas that align with your spiritual gifts.

But whether you're already serving within your gifting, investigating your spiritual gifts for the first time, or anywhere in between, our ministry prays that this book and its online assessment help you discover the unique gifts God has given you so that you might bring glory to him and further his mission in the world around you.

TAKE OUR SPIRITUAL GIFTS ASSESSMENT

Our gifts are tools from God, intended to help us and others grow in our walk with him, but far too often they go underappreciated and under-recognized. Part of the reason is that it can be easy to assume that you are gifted in whatever way you are currently serving.

The reality is, however, that the needs of our church or of those around us do not necessarily constitute our calling. And while that doesn't mean we should only serve in the areas where we are gifted, understanding the ways in which you can best align your God-given abilities with the needs of the kingdom can help you find a sense of joy and purpose in serving him that can otherwise be missing in our lives.

So, if you haven't already, please complete the free spiritual gift assessment offered by our ministry at **WhatAreMySpiritualGifts.com.**

Ideally, we ask that you take it yourself and then have a close friend, spouse, or someone else who knows you well take it with you in mind. Getting feedback from multiple sources can help provide a sense of clarity and depth to your understanding of where God has gifted you, though ultimately God's opinion is the one that matters most.

So, while no test is perfect, the results will at least give you a better understanding of your gifts and how they might work together.

Knowing your gifting, however, is of little importance unless it is paired with the knowledge of how to use them well. With that in mind, let's take a closer look at what the Bible says about spiritual gifts in general before diving into each individually.

WHAT DOES THE BIBLE SAY ABOUT SPIRITUAL GIFTS?

1 Corinthians 12:12–31: Your gifts are for God's glory

The passage of Scripture most often used when discussing spiritual gifts is 1 Corinthians 12:12–31. Here we find Paul's statement that every Christian has been gifted in a unique way and that it is vital we use those gifts according to God's calling since that is the only way the Body of Christ can function as the Lord intends.

In many ways, this lesson is the continuation of a theme that runs throughout much of the letter, and that context is important for understanding both how Paul talks about spiritual gifts and how we should see our individual gifts within the larger body of believers.

For example, in the previous chapter of 1 Corinthians, Paul describes division in the church because the wealthy Christians were consuming all the food and wine at the Lord's Supper before the poor Christians could get there. It's essentially a depiction of the wealthy using something meant to honor God to bring them all together for selfish reasons.

By pivoting from that passage to a discussion about spiritual gifts, Paul drives home that our gifts, like every other part of our lives, are meant to be used for God's glory rather than our own. The Lord has given us the freedom to choose the extent to which we'll live in accordance with those priorities, but he is also clear that there are consequences for making the wrong choice.

If we forget why we've been gifted in the first place, then it's easy to begin viewing those gifts through a more selfish lens. No gift is any more vital or God-inspired than the rest, but that's how it can appear if we take a worldly view of our spiritual blessings. That's why Paul writes about gifts in the context of the larger community of faith.

That corporate perspective on our personal gifts is an important message and one rightfully used to encourage believers. However, that's not the end of the conversation for Paul.

1 Corinthians 12:4–11: Your gifts are empowered by the Holy Spirit

Rather, he reached that point after first spending several verses describing the nature of spiritual gifts in general. In 1 Corinthians 12:4–11, he notes that every such gift—and the ones named in these verses do not form an exhaustive list—comes from the Holy Spirit and that these gifts must be empowered by the Spirit in order to function correctly.

The Greek word used in verse 11 to describe that empowerment is *energeo* and it literally means "to energize" or "to be at work." The basic idea is that our spiritual gifts can't work as God intends unless they are consistently powered by the Holy Spirit's presence in our lives.

That emphasis on how the gifts work best is important because our gifts don't magically appear at the moment of our salvation. Nor do they go away entirely if we're not walking with the Lord. Rather, God gave you your gifts when he knit you together in your mother's womb. They've always been part of your life and, typically, correspond pretty closely to your personality. While ranking low on a particular gift does not mean the Lord cannot use you in that capacity, all of us have some gifts that come more naturally than others. For example, regardless of your score on evangelism, you are still called to share your faith, but it could be that you would benefit from the example of those with this gift to know how to do so.

You see, God had a plan for the role he wanted you to play in his kingdom from the very beginning, and he gifted you to fill that role well. Those gifts, however, weren't fully actualized until the Holy Spirit came into your life. And they will not remain optimized apart from the Spirit's power.

Galatians 5:1–15: Gifts can be rendered idle

Paul gives us more insight into why that's the case in Galatians 5.

In this chapter, Paul uses circumcision to talk about the larger issue of self-justification. The notion that people had to earn their salvation—or justify God's free gift of it after being saved—was a big problem in the early church. The Jews built much of their society around the idea of following the law well enough to attain the Lord's favor, and that idea carried over into the first generations of Christians as well.

It's a heresy that Paul had to deal with in most of the places where he ministered, and he writes about it frequently because people who held that belief would often corrupt the churches he started after he had moved on to plant others.

By the time he wrote Galatians, you can tell he was fed up with that heresy. And a big part of his frustration was that the principle of self-justification tended to corrupt every facet of a believer's walk with God, including their spiritual gifts. In verse 4 he describes why that's the case: those who continue to try and justify themselves before God "are severed from Christ . . . you have fallen away from grace."

That phrase is a bit misleading in English, though. The Greek word used here for "severed" (*katargeo*) more literally translates as "to make idle." The idea is not that believers are in danger of losing their salvation; rather, they've rendered the life-giving grace of God inactive. They've essentially hit the off switch on their connection to the Holy Spirit. And, as Paul made clear in 1 Corinthians, our spiritual gifts can't function the way God intends unless the Spirit is the one making them work.

Galatians 5:16–21: Sin inhibits the Spirit's power

However, trying to justify our own standing before the Lord and power our own spiritual gifts is not the only way we can sever our connection to the Holy Spirit. Later on in Galatians 5, Paul describes another mistake believers can make to reach the same place spiritually.

In verses 16–21, Paul describes people who think they have a relationship with God but whose lives don't reflect his presence. He frames the discussion as a battle between the Spirit and the flesh, noting that one cannot serve both. His focus, however, is less on individual sins—though he is clear that no sin should be taken lightly—and more on the habitual kind.

In this passage, Paul is referencing those whose lifestyles are still defined by the sins of their former lives. Such sins inhibit the Holy Spirit's influence on a person and, as with those who try to justify themselves, the implication is that one's gifts will lack the Spirit's power.

Paul goes so far as to warn that those who lack the Spirit's power as described in these passages should examine whether or not they are actually saved (Galatians 5:19–21). While Scripture is clear that it's not our responsibility to judge the status of another person's salvation—only the individual and God can truly know that—Jesus did give us some basic guidelines when he talked about how a tree is recognized by its fruit (Matthew 7:15–19).

Galatians 5:22–23: The fruit of the Spirit and your spiritual gifts work in tandem

Paul gives us a bit more insight into what that fruit looks like toward the end of Galatians 5.

In verses 22–23, he writes that "the fruit of the Spirit is love, joy, peace, patience, kindness, goodness, faithfulness, gentleness, self-control." This fruit (collective, not singular) is a vital part of living out the spiritual gifts God has given us, but each characteristic will only be present in our lives when we are walking with the Spirit.

After all, some of the spiritual gifts can be pretty rotten without the fruit of the Spirit.

- Discernment without gentleness and kindness devolves into judgment.

- Evangelism without love becomes condemnation.
- Giving without faithfulness is done for our glory instead of God's.
- Serving without joy and peace does little to advance the gospel or minister to other people.
- Leadership without gentleness and self-control turns people into tyrants.

And the same basic principle applies to every one of the spiritual gifts.

Conversely, if we are connected to the Spirit, then our gifts will function as they should because they will be supported by the fruit of his presence in our lives.

- Shepherding with patience leads to discipleship.
- Hospitality with joy and kindness makes others feel welcome.
- Exhortation with love and goodness helps people accept your message.
- Mercy with peace and gentleness helps the hurting find comfort.

God designed our gifts to work in conjunction with the character and qualities his Spirit develops in those who walk with him. But if we let him, Satan will use for evil what God intends for good. While the Lord can still redeem our mistakes and bring a measure of blessing out of them, the kingdom would be much better off if he didn't have to.

YOUR NEXT STEPS

With that perspective in mind, let's continue by looking more closely at each of the spiritual gifts.

For the purposes of this study, I've divided seventeen spiritual gifts seen in the Bible into three categories based on the ways in which they often function within the body of Christ:

- the public gifts
- the personal gifts
- the paradigm gifts

Note: the sign gifts (e.g., healing and speaking in tongues) are not included in the test but are discussed in an article at WhatAreMySpiritualGifts.com.

While the Bible does not categorize them as such, I believe it's helpful to show how interrelated many of the gifts are and highlights the ways in which each of our gifts function in partnership with other believers as part of the larger body of Christ.

As mentioned previously, none of the gifts are inherently better or more important than the others. And it is not uncommon for people to be gifted in multiple areas.

As such, there is a benefit to learning about each of the spiritual gifts covered in this book. Just because a gift does not appear in your top three does not mean God will never call you to use it.

Moreover, understanding what each gift looks like in practice can help us gain a better understanding of how to recognize it in ourselves and in others. That said, if you would like to start with the gifts for which the Lord has given you the greatest affinity, I can't say that I blame you. Regardless of how you choose to proceed from here, please take the time to read the introductions for the sections in which your gifts appear before moving on to specifics about those individual gifts. They are included to explain why the gifts are organized as they are in this book and to provide context for the gifts that fit within that category.

And remember, how the Lord has chosen to gift you and the ways in which he plans to use those gifts for the kingdom are as unique as you are. So, as we move forward, proceed with an open heart and an attentive mind, asking the Spirit to help you process and understand both the nature of these gifts and the ways in which they apply to your life.

THE PUBLIC GIFTS

While all spiritual gifts are meant to have applications that extend beyond yourself in order to help build up the larger body of Christ, the public gifts are those that are most often practiced among other people. Their primary function cannot be fulfilled without involving others which, in turn, necessitates a communal context for their application. If your primary gifting is in one of these areas, know that the Lord's calling for you will involve working with those God brings into your life.

Public gifts include:

- Administration: Organizing people and ministries effectively
- Apostleship: Adapting to a different culture to share the gospel or do ministry

- Leadership: Motivating and inspiring others to serve Jesus fully
- Music: Sharing God's truth and love through music with unusual effectiveness
- Prophecy: Proclaiming the word of God with personal passion and effectiveness
- Teaching: Explaining God's word and truth with unusual effectiveness

It is also possible—if not probable—that you will have giftings in other areas. Moreover, even though each of these gifts is most commonly used in community with other people, their practical application may not look the same for everyone.

There are multiple ways, for example, to demonstrate the spiritual gift of leadership. Teachers often differ in their style, delivery, and methods of preparation. And some with the spiritual gift of music will lead from the front while others may exhibit that gifting in how they provide the necessary framework for others to lead people into a worshipful encounter with the Lord. Regardless of how the Holy Spirit uses your particular gifts, though, if they fall into this category, then working with others will be an important part of fulfilling your calling from the Lord.

As we prepare to look at each of these gifts in greater detail, remember that only God gets the final say regarding the particulars of how your gifts are supposed to be used. Keep an open mind, paying more attention to the general principles that comprise what it means to live out your gifting in community with others than to trying to fit your gifts into any particular mold.

And pray that the Holy Spirit will help any truths in these pages that is of particular relevance to your life and calling resonate in a way that helps you grow in your walk with him and your understanding of how he wants your gifts to be used.

ADMINISTRATION

Organizing people and ministries effectively

It can be hard to fully appreciate the importance of the spiritual gift of administration until it's missing. When those God has equipped and called to be administrators are present and doing their jobs well, it helps everyone else's responsibilities seem more manageable. The details run more smoothly and people are freed up to work within their respective giftings at a far greater capacity.

However, administration may not always feel like a gift for those who have it. Being good at coordinating people and helping an organization run smoothly can be a relatively thankless job. Often, you're noticed more when things go wrong than when they go right.

It can be easy for others to take the contributions of an administrator for granted. That unfortunate reality is why those who do not have the gift of administration should make a concerted effort to show appreciation for those who do. That's also why it's so important for those gifted in administration to find their joy and fulfillment in the praise of the Lord rather than from others.

Few people in the Bible exemplified that truth better than Nehemiah.

NEHEMIAH

Nehemiah served as cupbearer to King Artaxerxes roughly one hundred years after Persia had defeated Babylon and King Cyrus had allowed the Israelites to return to Jerusalem. Nehemiah's position was one of great importance and demonstrated the high regard in which he was held within the Persian court. However, despite his prominence within the Persian empire, his heart still broke for his people when he was told about the degraded state of Jerusalem.

He felt a burden from the Lord to go back and help, so he asked the king for a leave of absence. Artaxerxes valued Nehemiah's abilities and contributions so much that he not only granted the request but also provided many of the resources necessary to rebuild the fallen parts of the city's defenses. Of course, it probably helped that Nehemiah was organized enough to know exactly what he needed and whom he would need to help him in order to accomplish that task.

From the start of his story, we see Nehemiah's gifting in action. And it's worth noting that God laid that burden on the heart of someone he had already equipped to carry it well. The poor state of Jerusalem was hardly a secret, but it was Nehemiah who seems to have felt God's call to help most acutely.

If you have the gift of administration, the same tends to be true of the instances when God calls you to step in and help. Oftentimes, the individual needs of a ministry or situation are evident to anyone who takes the time to look. But it is frequently those with the gift of administration who see how those needs intersect and understand how to organize people to meet them.

Nehemiah exhibited this aspect of his gifting once again upon reaching Jerusalem.

After spending a few days and nights assessing the situation, Nehemiah approached the leaders of Jerusalem and shared his vision for rebuilding the city's walls, as well as the stories of how the Persian king had blessed his mission. He then helped to organize them into groups that set about the task of rebuilding the primary gates, many of which had remained in a state of disrepair since Babylon had crushed the city and sent the Israelites into exile. After that, they shored up the gaps in the walls that left Jerusalem vulnerable to attack until everything was rebuilt and the city was secure once again (Nehemiah 2–5).

In total, it took them less than two months to accomplish the task that had been left undone for more than a century. And while the king did supply some of the necessary resources, the key was Nehemiah's ability to organize the people in such a way that the otherwise overwhelming amount of work seemed manageable. After all, the vast majority of those who rebuilt Jerusalem's walls and gates had been there for years. They just needed someone to help them know how to do the work that they could all agree needed to be done.

Nehemiah was gifted and called to that purpose, and his faithfulness positioned him to be used by God to accomplish something remarkable.

It's worth noting, however, that throughout this process they faced opposition from those who wanted to keep the city weak. Men like Sanballat, Tobiah, and Geshem repeatedly tried to undermine Nehemiah's plans (Nehemiah 2:19), threatened to attack the Israelites in the middle of their labor (4:7–8), and even plotted to kill Nehemiah because his approach proved so effective (6:1–2).

And it's not hard to imagine that even those who did their part within the structure provided by Nehemiah had their moments of doubts. Nehemiah, however, remained committed to the work and found his sense of purpose and joy in knowing that what he was doing was in line with God's call.

IF YOU HAVE THE SPIRITUAL GIFT OF ADMINISTRATION

Sometimes those with the gift of administration are called to exercise their abilities on the public stage like Nehemiah. Just as often, though, organizing groups and people to be better optimized in the work God has called you to do will go relatively unnoticed by others. They may even resent any limitations that come with the perception of being told how to do their job. That's why it's vital that you find your confidence and calling in the Lord rather than in the opinions of others. However, that's also why it's so important to make sure that this gift is used in conjunction with the fruit of the Spirit.

After all, sometimes the reason people resent being organized in a particular way is that the one doing the organizing is trying to impose unnecessary burdens or restrict their creativity. At other times, the motivations may be pure, but the messaging lacks the necessary kindness and gentleness to convey the plan well.

Ultimately, you must learn to exercise your gift of administration in a way that embodies the character of Christ, or even the most genuine and well-intentioned efforts can fall short of accomplishing God's will. But when administration is done well, few spiritual gifts can make as large of an impact on an organization or group of people as an administrator with the ability to optimize everyone else's gifts and callings.

APOSTLESHIP

*Adapting to a different culture to share the
gospel or do ministry*

The spiritual gift of apostleship is, in many ways, similar to that of evangelism. In both cases, the focus of the gift is on sharing the gospel with those who need to hear it. When Paul writes about spiritual gifts in Ephesians, though, he separates the apostles and evangelists, describing both as distinct giftings within the body of Christ (Ephesians 4:11).

So what's the difference?

Evangelism is discussed at greater length in its own chapter, but the key distinction seems to be that evangelism can—and should—occur in any setting while the spiritual gift of apostleship is granted to those God wants to use to share his good news in different cultures. In Greek, the word *apostolos* conveys the sense of an envoy or an individual commissioned to go and represent the one who sent him or her.

In the biblical context, that means someone who is sent out by God to share his good news in an environment other than his or her own. To enable those with this calling to accomplish that task, the Holy Spirit gives them a unique ability to adapt to different settings and contextualize the gospel message in a way others can understand without losing themselves or God's truth in the process.

That last part is especially important. It's also why Paul offers us an excellent example of what it means to live out the spiritual gift of apostleship well.

PAUL THE APOSTLE

Throughout Acts and Paul's letters, we see Paul embody the mission of an apostle in the sense of being sent out by God to share the gospel in other cultures. In Acts 9, God describes to Ananias how Paul is "a chosen instrument of mine to carry my name before the Gentiles and kings and the children of Israel" (Acts 9:15). Beginning with the church in Antioch, Paul spent the rest of his life doing just that. And while the book of Acts and Paul's letters detail that endeavor well, he sums up his approach best in his first letter to the church in Corinth.

While detailing the ways in which he's been an apostle to the Corinthians and defending his work amongst them, Paul writes,

> For though I am free from all, I have made myself a servant to all, that I might win more of them. To the Jews I became as a Jew, in order to win Jews. To those under the law I became as one under the law (though not being myself under the law) that I might win those under the law. To those outside the law I became as one outside the law (not being outside the law of God but under the law of Christ) that I might win those outside the law. To the weak I became weak, that I might win the weak. I have become all things to all people, that by all means I might save some. I do it all for the sake of the gospel, that I may share with them in its blessings (1 Corinthians 9:19–23).

For Paul, the only nonnegotiables were his identity in Christ and the truth of God's word. Beyond those two core aspects of his mission, he understood that the rest could adapt to his context. He didn't need Gentiles to become Jews or the weak to become strong because God didn't need that. Rather, the Lord tasked Paul with taking his message to people where they were in order to help them know him better.

That said, he also understood that the fundamental truth of the gospel did not need to change. While Paul was more than willing to contextualize himself, he never watered down or altered the good news he preached. Every message was centered on Jesus and the salvation that is available only through him. Whether he was preaching to Jews in a synagogue, to philosophers in the Areopagus, or to merchants in the town square, Paul refused to compromise the centrality of Christ and the necessity of placing one's faith in him as the only path to salvation.

IF YOU HAVE THE SPIRITUAL GIFT OF APOSTLESHIP

If you have the spiritual gift of apostleship today, finding that balance between adapting your presentation of the gospel without altering the truth of the gospel remains an essential part of living out your calling well. In addition, understanding what parts of your identity can change with your context without losing sight of who you are in Christ is also an indispensable component of your gifting. Fortunately, the same Holy Spirit that created you for that purpose stands ready to empower you to fulfill it.

Relying on God's help to live out your gifting will be an everyday necessity because every day will present you with opportunities to take a seemingly easier path. In fact, one of the chief dangers against which you must guard is losing track of those lines that you cannot afford to cross.

Shifting your view on the reality of the resurrection, for example, may yield short-term gains if one of the barriers to belief is the idea of miracles. In the same way, relaxing the moral standards taught by Christ on any number of subjects could make our savior appear more appealing to someone who does not want to change their own behavior or risk running afoul of what's considered culturally acceptable. But when you start to compromise the essentials of the gospel, you also compromise its savior and risk inviting people into a relationship with a god of your own making rather than with Jesus Christ.

A second danger is becoming so enamored with the prospect of sharing the gospel in other cultures that you lose sight of the fact that there are also lost people where you are who may need your help as well. If you have the spiritual gift of apostleship, then your primary calling may very well be to take his good news to a foreign country and establish churches where none currently exist. However, you don't have to go across the world to find other cultures in need of God's truth.

It could be that part of your calling is to foster ministry cooperation in a multiracial setting or work with those of a different socioeconomic class to help them understand that the gospel doesn't belong to any one people group. Perhaps you have been given the gift of apostleship to help guide your community of faith to start looking a bit more like the one John saw in heaven (Revelation 7:9–10).

If you have the spiritual gift of apostleship, know that there are a variety of ways that the Lord may call you to use it. But whether it's across the world or just across your city, your ability to help people from different cultures and backgrounds see that the good news of Jesus is relevant for them is an essential part of helping the body of Christ fulfill the mission of Christ to the glory of God.

LEADERSHIP

*Motivating and inspiring others to serve
Jesus fully*

To an extent, most people are called to lead someone. Parents are meant to lead their children. Husbands are meant to lead their wives. Mature Christians are meant to lead those newer to the faith. To that end, leadership is a crucial ability for everyone to develop. However, there is an important distinction between someone who is required to lead and someone who has been spiritually gifted to lead.

Those required to lead—which can include those gifted in this area as well—usually do so because the nature of their situation or role leaves them in a position where people are prone to follow their example. It could be in a job where people work beneath you in the company hierarchy or in a family where others look to you for guidance. However, most of us can think of examples where the person who was supposed to lead was neither equipped nor capable of doing so well.

And therein lies the difference between those required to lead and those gifted to lead.

Individuals with the spiritual gift of leadership often find themselves inspiring others to follow their example regardless of their role in a given situation. It's the coworker who sets the tone at the office, even when he or she isn't the boss. It's the friend whom people look to when something goes wrong or when the group can't decide what to do. And it's the family member who seems to have the ability to step into a debate or squabble and be a voice of reason and calm. At least, that's the case when the spiritual gift of leadership is exercised well.

After all, it's also quite possible for those who have been gifted and called to lead to do so in a way that breeds disharmony and conflict wherever they go. Those with this gift often lead even when they shouldn't because they have a natural ability to engender support from those around them. That's why it's so important to make sure that if you have the spiritual gift of leadership, you use it in the power and guidance of the Holy Spirit.

As we see with the example of Josiah in the Bible, when you lead well, you can make an enormous difference for God's kingdom and in the lives of those around you.

KING JOSIAH

Josiah was eight years old when he became king of Judah and, as is often the case throughout the books of 1 and 2 Kings, he is defined first and foremost by the degree to which he did what was right in the eyes of the Lord.

Josiah was one of the few who followed God well, which is made all the more impressive by the fact that there was little about the way his predecessors ruled that made following God easy. You see, Josiah was the grandson of Manasseh—perhaps the worst ruler that Judah ever had—and the son of Amon, who was not much better. Josiah became king at such a young age because those before him had left Judah in such a bad state that his father was killed in his own home by those who conspired against him (2 Kings 21).

The people of the land then made Josiah king, and little changed initially. However, in the eighteenth year of his reign, he decided to renovate the Temple and the priest Hilkiah stumbled across the Book of the Law. It was eventually read to the king and, in response, Josiah "tore his clothes" and ordered that the priests "inquire of the LORD for me, and for the people, and for all of Judah, concerning the words of this book that have been found.

For great is the wrath of the Lord that is kindled against us, because our fathers have not obeyed the words of this book, to do according to all that is written concerning us" (2 Kings 22:11–13).

God's answer was that his wrath would be poured out on Judah eventually, but his punishment would wait because Josiah had humbled himself and had a penitent heart when he learned of the wrongs that had been committed (vv. 15–20).

The king, however, was not content with simply knowing that he would not face God's judgment. So, in response, he brought together representatives from across Judah and led all the people of Jerusalem to the Temple, where he read the Book of the Covenant to them (2 Kings 23:1–2). He then "made a covenant before the LORD, to walk after the LORD and to keep his commandments and his testimonies and his statutes with all his heart and all his soul, to perform the words of this covenant that were written in this book. And all the people joined in the covenant" (v. 3).

He then put actions to his words by commanding the priests and keepers of the Temple to bring out all the pagan idols and burn them outside the city walls (v. 4). After that was done, he got rid of all the pagan priests that previous kings had put in place, broke down the houses of the male cult prostitutes that were in the house of the Lord, and tore down the high places where pagan sacrifices were offered (v. 5–20). Once Judah was cleansed of its idolatry, he then led them to observe the first Passover since the time of the Judges, a practice that was missing even during the reign of notable kings like David and Solomon (v. 21–23).

The account of his actions concludes with the note that "there was no king like him, who turned to the Lord with all his heart and with all his soul and with all his might, according to all the Law of Moses, nor did any like him arise after him" (v. 25). And while Judah still eventually suffered the same fate as Israel when subsequent kings returned to the sinful ways of their forefathers, at least for a time Josiah led God's people back into a right standing with the Lord.

That is the power of the spiritual gift of leadership when used in service to God.

IF YOU HAVE THE SPIRITUAL GIFT OF LEADERSHIP

If you have the spiritual gift of leadership, know that you don't have to be a king or even a person in authority for God to use it to help others grow in their walk with him. While much of what Josiah was able to accomplish was due to his position as king, the principles by which he went about leading Judah are replicable in a variety of circumstances.

To start, he understood that before he could lead others to pursue a right relationship with God, he had to be right with God. Recall that his first response upon hearing the law read was personal repentance. Only after he had repented of his own sins and spiritual negligence did he try to lead others to do the same.

If you have the spiritual gift of leadership, know that people are likely to look to you as an example regardless of whether you deserve that attention. As such, it is profoundly important that you remember to prioritize your own relationship with the Lord, even if it seems like the requirements of leading others make finding the time to do so difficult.

Fortunately, because people are often drawn to those with this gifting, the most natural way to lead them to God is often by simply following him yourself. One of Paul's most effective means of leadership is summed up well in this statement: "Be imitators of me, as I am of Christ" (1 Corinthians 11:1). For those with the spiritual gift of leadership, that approach can often bear remarkable fruit.

As Josiah reminds us, however, God will often call those with this gift to do more than just live out their faith publicly. Once he knew that he was right with God, he took the necessary steps to help others make the same decision. It was not enough to know that he would avoid the Lord's judgment. As the leader of his people, he felt responsible for doing everything in his power to help them grow as well. And he did so in such a way that he engendered the support of his people despite asking them to make some truly radical changes.

Josiah led them to undo generations of sinful behaviors and practices. Moreover, many of these actions required a level of faith in him and the truth he called them to hold that, if he was wrong, threatened their very existence. After all, they had adopted the worship of other gods because they'd lost faith in the true God to protect and provide for them. Going back to God now, when it had been at least seventy-five years since they'd last worshiped him alone, must have been daunting, to say the least.

Yet, that is the power of the spiritual gift of leadership in practice. And if you have this gift, know that God can use you in the same way he used Josiah. Your calling may not be to lead an entire nation back to the Lord, but what about your church or your office? What about your neighbors or your home?

If you have been given this gift, people are likely to follow you wherever you may lead. So embrace that responsibility and remember that, while it may manifest in a variety of ways, it is always given for the same ultimate purpose: leading others to know and serve God.

Use it well.

MUSIC

Sharing God's truth and love through music in a way that draws people into a personal encounter with him

To begin, it's important to note that musical talent and the spiritual gift of music are different, and that basic truth is not an indictment of either. God gives musical ability to a variety of people and delights when they use it to his glory. But the spiritual gift of music is granted to those through whom the Holy Spirit works to use that ability to draw people into a worshipful encounter with the Lord.

If you took the spiritual gifts assessment and were surprised by your score in this category, take that as an indication that perhaps you need to spend some time in prayer, asking God to help you understand your results a bit better.

For those with musical ability, it can be easy to grow up being told, or simply assuming, that you are meant to use those skills to lead worship. However, the encouragement of other people does not always equate with the calling of the Lord, and there are a variety of ways that he can use your talents. Again, having musical ability but not the spiritual gift of music should not be seen as a negative. It just means God may have other plans for your abilities.

For others, it could be that you have the spiritual gift of music but have been uncertain of how to use it because you have never been the most naturally talented musician. If that sounds like you, know that there are a variety of ways God can use your gift. It could be that you are meant to lead a worship team but to do so from the background. You could have a gift for writing music that inspires others to walk closer with the Lord. This gift can manifest in many ways, but those who have it need to keep an open mind to make sure that the Holy Spirit is the one directing its use.

But if this gift does not always appear in the way we might expect, how should we understand it, and how can you know if it's something that the Holy Spirit has given you? Let's start by taking a look at one of the most notable spiritually gifted musicians within the pages of Scripture.

KING DAVID

King David is famous for many reasons, but his musical abilities are often chief among them. He was a talented musician, renowned for his ability with the harp and his poetic lyricism. However, being able to string together notes and words in a way that others found pleasing is not how he demonstrates this spiritual gift.

Rather, it is seen most clearly in the way that, through the psalms he wrote, he has been leading people into a worshipful encounter with God for the better part of three thousand years. The honesty and transparency with which he wrote have helped people expand their understanding of how to relate to God, while the praise he offers the Lord continues to echo in the hearts and minds of believers even now. Those whom the Holy Spirit inspires to write powerful lyrics and songs today manifest this gift in a similar way.

Beyond the psalms, David also led people to worship the Lord by setting an example for them to follow. When he led the procession that brought the ark of the covenant back to Jerusalem, for example, he began by "celebrating before the Lord, with songs and lyres and harps and tambourines and castanets and cymbals" (2 Samuel 6:5). And while the death of Uzzah caused him to mistakenly leave the ark with Obed-edom for a time, when he eventually returned to carry it all the way back, that procession continued. The people of God worshiped the Lord because they saw David doing so. His actions inspired others to enter into God's presence, and the same is often true today for those with the spiritual gift of music.

A final way that this gift manifested in David's life was on a more personal level. One of the first jobs David had after leaving his father's sheep was working in the court of Saul as the king's personal musician. After God's favor departed from Saul, he began to be plagued by "a harmful spirit from the LORD" that would drive him to depression and bouts of insanity (1 Samuel 16:14). (Such spirits were how mental illness was commonly understood in biblical times).

In response, Saul's servants recommended that he find someone to play music in the hopes that it might help his condition. David was eventually recommended because he was "skillful in playing" and, most importantly, "the LORD is with him" (v. 18). So David was summoned and "whenever the harmful spirit from God was upon Saul, David took the lyre and played it with his hand. So Saul was refreshed and was well, and the harmful spirit departed from him" (v. 23).

Now, it would be a mistake to equate the spiritual gift of music with the ability to perform musical exorcisms. However, it speaks to the spirit within David and the way that God used his gifts that, when he played for Saul, it imparted the peace of God to the troubled king. In the same way, one of the most impactful ways that the Holy Spirit empowers the spiritual gift of music is to remove the barriers that can make it difficult for people to fully engage with God in worship.

If you've ever been sitting in a church service or listening to a song, but not really paying attention, only for something in the melody or lyrics to snap you out of the fog and cut straight to your heart, then you've experienced something akin to what David did for Saul. After all, you don't have to have an evil spirit or mental illness to get distracted or for the problems of the day to take up the bulk of your attention. God can use those with the spiritual gift of music to help people focus on him in a way that fosters a genuine connection with the Lord.

IF YOU HAVE THE SPIRITUAL GIFT OF MUSIC

If you have the spiritual gift of music, the Holy Spirit can use your gift in a variety of ways to share God's love and truth while drawing people into a personal encounter with the Lord. As such, it is important for those with this gift to keep an open mind on how God might want to use your gift.

One of the primary dangers against which you'll need to guard is thinking that because the Lord used your gift in one way, that's how he will always want to use it. For example, if you have led worship at your church or in a group setting, it can be easy to think that you are always supposed to lead worship. It could be that a time will come when the Holy Spirit chooses to call someone else to fill that role instead and you are meant to either continue from the background or to serve as a mentor to that person.

God could also want you to focus on your other gifts for a time in a way that is incompatible with your former role. Remaining flexible with how you understand your gift of music and allowing the Lord to be the one in charge of directing its use is essential to making sure that the body of Christ functions as it should. It's also the best way to guard against your gift beginning to seem more like an obligation than an opportunity, which often leads to a second danger to keep in mind.

A second risk you will have to watch out for if you have the spiritual gift of music is becoming so confident in your talents that you forget to rely on the Holy Spirit to empower them. One of the ways that can happen is when you continue exercising your gifts as you always have when God has called you to pivot to something else. It can be a subtle shift over time, and your talents can often mean that the end product will be similar enough that others might not notice. But the joy, passion, and purpose with which you once exercised your gifting will begin to fade until you find yourself performing for others rather than guiding them into an encounter with the Lord.

That danger can also manifest when the focus of your music shifts from God to yourself. Again, that change will likely happen gradually over time. However, if your identity becomes based on your performance and talents rather than on your relationship with the Lord, it's easy for music to become more than a tool God can use to draw people to himself and instead grow into the primary way that you derive value and meaning in your life. At that point, it has ceased to be a gift and has instead become an impediment to your walk with the Lord.

When used in the power and guidance of the Holy Spirit, the spiritual gift of music can draw people to God in a unique and compelling way. It can help God's truth resonate in a way that the spoken word may not. And it can embed the Lord's love deep within a person's heart and mind.

If you have the spiritual gift of music, remember that your gift does not belong to you. Instead, surrender it back to the Lord each time you use it. If you will, then the Holy Spirit can work through your life to accomplish amazing things for God's kingdom.

PROPHECY

*Proclaiming the word of God with
personal passion and effectiveness*

Of all the spiritual gifts, prophecy is perhaps the most misunderstood. After all, often when people think of the prophets, stories of Ezekiel cooking with dung (Ezekiel 4:12), Hosea marrying a prostitute who cheated on him constantly (Hosea 3:1–5), and Isaiah walking around naked for three years (Isaiah 20:1–4) are what come to mind first. If that's what it means to have the spiritual gift of prophecy, then it's understandable that people would be wary of it.

Fortunately, the weird stuff they did is not what made them prophets. Rather, their passionate deliverance of God's word commanded people's attention. And while those messages did, at times, portend a future judgment or describe events that were going to happen, most of the time biblical prophecy is a word from God for the culture at the time it's given rather than for some distant date. Even when the Lord's message included a note about something that would not come to pass for hundreds of years, it often had a sense of power and purpose that was of immediate relevance to those who heard it.

When Paul writes of the spiritual gift of prophecy in his letters, that idea of proclaiming a word from God to a culture that needs to hear it is what he meant. And doing so often requires the same kind of courage and conviction that the biblical prophets demonstrated throughout their lives. We see those qualities and the way the Holy Spirit uses them clearly in the example of Nathan.

THE PROPHET NATHAN

Nathan was a powerful and respected prophet during the reigns of David and Solomon. He lived a good life, and tradition teaches that he died of old age rather than as a result of a king's wrath.

Still, he is most famous in Scripture for the times he was willing to risk that wrath in order to convey a message from the Lord.

The first such instance takes place in 2 Samuel 7, when David decided that he wanted to build a Temple because he didn't feel right about having a better home than the ark of the covenant. So he mentioned his plan to Nathan, and Nathan initially agreed that it was a good idea. Later that night, however, God appeared to Nathan and told him David was not fit to build the Temple because of all the blood he'd shed (1 Chronicles 22:8).

God also told Nathan that he appreciated David's intentions, would give him rest from his enemies, and establish his line forever. But the prophet still had to tell the king that God wanted someone else to build the Temple (2 Samuel 7:4–17). Overall, though, that wasn't the scariest message to present. That honor is reserved for the second time we see Nathan in action.

When David's story is told, the low point is when he impregnates Bathsheba, has her husband killed, and then marries her to pretend that the baby was not conceived in sin. And, for a time, it appears that the king got away with his sinful behavior. Few knew of the initial affair, and there was no way to prove who the child's father was when the baby came into the picture. God knew, though, and he tasked Nathan with confronting the man who had already killed one person to hide his sin.

So, knowing the risk he was taking when appearing before the king, Nathan started with a story.

He told David of a rich man who stole the only lamb that a poor man owned because the rich man was not content with or willing to share from his own abundant flock. David immediately declared that the rich man should have to pay fourfold for the lamb he stole and that he deserved to die for his sin. Then "Nathan said to David, 'You are the man!'" (2 Samuel 12:1–7).

The prophet then proceeded to relay a message from the Lord reminding the king of all that God had done for him, before concluding with the warning that "the sword shall never depart from your house, because you have despised me and have taken the wife of Uriah the Hittite to be your wife" along with the promise that "I will raise up evil against you out of your own house . . . For you did it secretly, but I will do this thing before all Israel and before the sun" (vv.8–12).

It was at this point that Nathan had good reason to expect the king's wrath to be poured out on him, just as it had been on Uriah. David had already proven what he was capable of doing when pushed, and Nathan had certainly pushed. Yet when faced with a word from God, the king instead responded by declaring "I have sinned against the LORD" and showed contrition for his mistakes (v. 13).

The lives of other prophets demonstrate that those with this spiritual gift should not expect their message from the Lord to always be received with that same degree of acceptance. Many were tortured and killed because they would not compromise the word of God to make it more palatable to its intended audience. Yet, in this instance, we see the power God's word can have when proclaimed with confidence and an authority born of the knowledge that the message you send comes from the Lord rather than yourself.

For those with the gift of prophecy, Nathan stands as a good example of what that gift often looks like in practice today.

IF YOU HAVE THE SPIRITUAL GIFT OF PROPHECY

If you have the spiritual gift of prophecy, know that it will not always be appreciated or accepted by those to whom God calls you to share his message. But also know that you will not find peace or joy in your walk with the Lord if you refuse to share the message that he gives you. As Jeremiah describes, "If I say, 'I will not mention him, or speak any more in his name,' there is in my heart as it were a burning fire shut up in my bones, and I am weary with holding it in, and I cannot" (Jeremiah 20:9).

One of the surest ways to know if you have the gift of prophecy is to reflect on the times when you received a genuine message from the Lord. Did it feel like something you had to share? That sense of urgency and purpose is a defining characteristic of the gift when it shows up in Scripture. However, knowing why you feel compelled to speak is just as important as that sense of urgency itself.

After all, the Bible is filled with examples of those who claimed to share God's message because they liked the response it got from others or because it gave them a feeling of personal significance. The false prophets that surrounded kings and frequently outnumbered God's chosen messengers prove that there will always be those willing to claim God's authority for their own words because they feel it will bring them power or attention. And even true prophets can make this mistake when they begin to act as though every word they share comes from the Lord. Even in biblical times, it was relatively rare for a person to be given a message from God that they felt confident in ascribing to him.

So if you have the spiritual gift of prophecy, it is vital that you make sure you're using it for the right reasons. It's also how you can distinguish your calling from those who would justify their own thoughts as God's because they think it will benefit them personally, which leads to a second danger against which you must guard.

A second threat comes from how you will be tempted to react to the way others respond to the message you present. Because there will be times when God's message is not received well and delivering it in accordance with his will carries a higher cost than you might prefer to pay, it can be easy for those with this gifting to become jaded and hard-hearted toward those the Lord is trying to save. As mentioned in the introduction, the spiritual gifts will not work properly unless they are imbued with the fruit of the spirit, and that's especially true for prophecy. If you attempt to practice your gifting without the Spirit's patience, love, and faithfulness—to name a few—then you are going to burn out and end up looking more like Jonah than Nathan.

If you have the spiritual gift of prophecy, there is joy to be found in declaring God's word to those who need to hear it. But if you are relying on anyone but the Lord to supply that joy, then you will fall short of his calling in your life or give in to the temptation to start sharing your own message instead.

So the next time you feel led by God to declare a word from him, take the time to prayerfully examine your motivations for doing so. Are your actions and message driven by the desire to share God's word with his intended audience? Are you willing to stand by your message even if it's unpopular? And are you sure that the words you ascribe to the Lord are actually from him?

If your answer to each of those questions is yes, then proceed with a sense of confidence and conviction born of the Holy Spirit's blessing. However, if you're not sure, then it's better to go back to God for confirmation than risk profaning his name with a message that has not come from him.

Our culture is in dire need of those willing and able to both hear a word from the Lord and then share it with others. If you have been called by God to this purpose, embrace that responsibility, but never forget the weight of it as well. It is not something you can bear on your own, but as long as you use your gift in the power of the Holy Spirit, you won't have to.

TEACHING

Explaining God's word and truth with unusual effectiveness

The spiritual gift of teaching is meant to give individuals the ability to explain God's word and truth to others with unusual effectiveness. The Holy Spirit loves to help anyone study Scripture and know how to apply it to their own lives. However, through those with the gift of teaching, he is able to accomplish that same purpose on a larger scale and, in the process, foster dialogue and conversation that helps those individual revelations build up the body of Christ on a broader scale.

The best example of the spiritual gift of teaching is seen in Jesus. While pointing to him may seem like cheating since he demonstrates almost every spiritual gift across the course of his ministry—we don't know much about his musical capacities—his Sermon on the Mount is the clearest example we have of how to impart biblical truth in a way that is both understandable and applicable to a given audience. Moreover, by contrasting God's truth with that of the religious leaders, he also demonstrates the difference between teaching from a place of spiritual gifting rather than human ability.

JESUS VS. THE RELIGIOUS LEADERS

The religious leaders in the time of Christ perfected how to serve God from a fallen, human point of view. They placed the utmost importance on the observance of his laws and created safeguard upon safeguard to ensure that people would not transgress them.

The gospels, however, are filled with examples of how God incarnate desires more from his people. To that end, in the Sermon on the Mount Jesus distills the fundamental truths of what it means to honor God's law while living in a manner he can use and bless. And he does so with such effectiveness that, when he was done, "the crowds were astonished at his teaching, for he was teaching them as one who had authority, and not as their scribes" (Matthew 7:28–29).

However, nothing of what Jesus said should have been new information. Rather, it was the *way* he taught that made it stand out, cutting through centuries of efforts to expand on God's truth with human wisdom. By framing his teachings against those of the religious leaders, Jesus demonstrates the difference between explaining God's word with God's guidance and attempting to do so on our own. Those efforts began with the beatitudes.

Contrary to the way in which the Law was presented by most religious leaders of his time, Jesus commenced his instruction on how to live with a focus on character rather than commands. And until we understand why, we'll never fully grasp the gravity of all the instruction that comes after. Even if we somehow managed to keep every command found in this sermon but did not exhibit the characteristics described in its first twelve verses, then we would never fully experience the blessing of God in our lives. (For more on that particular aspect, read Dr. Jim Denison's book, *Blessed: Eight Ways Christians Change Culture*.)

From there, Jesus continued by reminding his disciples that this emphasis on character in no way detracted from the importance of right action. Across the rest of the sermon, he reframed the way his audience should understand subjects like anger, lust, promises, and relating to their enemies (Matthew 5:21–48) while also reorienting the way they were to approach serving God through giving, prayer, and fasting (Mathew 6:1–24). He concluded his teaching with lessons on trusting the Lord (Matthew 6:25–7:12) and obeying his commands (Matthew 7:13–27), which could now be understood in the larger context of God's will rather than in accordance with the dogmatic and misguided laws of the religious leaders.

By the end of his sermon, Jesus had deconstructed the errors within the existing law to instead allow God's word to be known and understood. And he did so in a way that, though it left the audience amazed, did not leave them confused. As a result, people have been going back to his words for nearly two thousand years because the truth contained within continues to resonate and transform lives.

IF YOU HAVE THE SPIRITUAL GIFT OF TEACHING

If you have the spiritual gift of teaching, know that you don't have to be Jesus to share his truth in a way that can draw people closer to God. If you are teaching within the power and guidance of the Holy Spirit, then the same power that helped his words resonate with the crowds on that mountainside can work through you as well. At the same time, it is far easier than we might care to admit for our teaching to fall more in line with the religious leaders than with Christ.

After all, most of the scribes and Pharisees were well-intentioned, devout, and learned people. They genuinely wanted to help people know God better and live within his blessing. And they taught to that end with an admirable sense of passion and purpose. It's just that, far too often, they forgot to include God in the conversation, opting instead to trust in their resources and the teachings of those who came before them.

If you have the spiritual gift of teaching, one of the dangers you must work hard to avoid is becoming so reliant on the resources from others that you forget that the Holy Spirit and the word of God must always be the beginning and end of your preparations. If you are teaching a passage from Scripture, start by spending time with God's word and in prayer instead of going straight to a provided lesson plan or commentary. Those can be useful resources, but if you want the Holy Spirit to speak through you to explain and apply his word to those you are teaching, then you need to give him the space to reveal his truth in that context.

When Jesus talked about the birds and plants as an analogy for God's provision, he was taking divine truth and applying it to the context of his audience (Matthew 6:25–34). If you want the Holy Spirit to do the same through you, then you have to give him the time and space to show you how his truth relates to those you are teaching.

At the same time, you must also guard against the temptation of becoming so reliant upon the Lord that you stop putting in the work yourself. Teaching God's word is meant to be a partnership between you and the Holy Spirit. While he is the one on whom you must rely for wisdom and guidance, he often imparts those lessons through your own personal study.

When Jesus promised that the Holy Spirit would tell his disciples what to say when they were brought before the synagogues and rulers, he did not mean that new information would magically pop into their heads (Luke 12:11–12). If you look at the way those interactions often played out, the disciples typically unpacked the Old Testament prophesies and the work of God among humanity in a way that pointed directly to Christ. While their application and understanding of that information was new and inspired by the Holy Spirit, they had spent their entire lives studying those stories and putting that information in their heads. When the time came to use it, God simply connected it in new ways to reveal his truth.

In the same way, if you have the spiritual gift of teaching, there may be times when you hear yourself saying things you'd never thought to say or discovering new lessons and connections in God's word that help to explain and apply his truth to your audience. Most often, though, those thoughts are new ways of understanding the information you already knew. While it is absolutely necessary to rely on the Holy Spirit to empower and guide your teaching, the more time you put into studying his word and reflecting on its truth before you get up to teach, the more he'll have to work with as you present your lesson and engage with others.

You don't have to have the spiritual gift of teaching to present God's word in a way that draws people closer to him. But if you do, know that the Holy Spirit has chosen to give you that ability to explain his truth with unusual effectiveness for a reason. So prayerfully look for opportunities to use it. While teaching is a gift, it is also a skill, and one that the Holy Spirit will continue to develop in you the more often you use it well. But do not take your gift for granted or forget its source.

The religious leaders were gifted teachers, but they could not change the hearts and minds of their audience in the same way as Jesus because they taught in their power rather than God's. The Lord has called you to a higher standard, and he stands ready to help you attain it.

Will you accept his help?

THE PERSONAL GIFTS

While every spiritual gift is meant to have some application and relevance to your life in particular, the personal gifts are those that often manifest in either your individual walk with the Lord or with a small group of people. That's not to say God can't use your gifts to help in a larger setting, but, for the most part, the gifts in this area work best in a more personal context. If your primary gifting is in one of these areas, being intentional about setting aside time to pour into your personal relationship with God and the individual or small group relationships into which he leads you will be essential to practicing your gifts well.

Personal gifts include:

- Discernment: Distinguishing truth from error or heresy
- Exhortation: Encouraging, comforting, and challenging others as they follow Jesus
- Knowledge: Understanding and sharing the deep truths of God's word and will (understanding)
- Shepherding: Helping others grow spiritually
- Wisdom: Relating biblical truth to practical life with great effectiveness (insights/applications)

It is also possible—if not probable—that you will have giftings in other areas. Moreover, even though each of these gifts is most commonly used in a smaller setting, their practical application may not look the same for everyone.

If you have the gift of shepherding, for example, there are multiple ways that God may call you to invest in discipling others. You might focus on one person for a time, only for the Lord to then call you to shepherd a small group of individuals. Likewise, the gifts of knowledge and wisdom could manifest as sharing the truths that God reveals to you with others, or they could be meant, for a time, just for you, in order to help you grow in your walk with the Lord. Regardless of how the Holy Spirit uses your particular gifts, though, if they fall into this category, then making time to hear from the Lord is vital to fulfilling God's purpose for your life.

As we prepare to look at each of these gifts in greater detail, remember that only God gets the final say regarding the particulars of how your gifts are supposed to be used.

Keep an open mind, paying more attention to the general principles that comprise what it means to live out your gifting than to trying to fit your gifts into any particular mold.

And pray that the Holy Spirit will help any truths in these pages that are of particular relevance to your life and calling resonate in a way that helps you grow in your walk with him and your understanding of how he wants your gifts to be used.

DISCERNMENT

Distinguishing truth from error or heresy

The spiritual gift of discernment may not always feel like a blessing. As we'll discuss in greater depth later in this chapter, discernment is often not appreciated by those around you. While that has always been true to some extent, our culture's current emphasis on personal truth and toleration has made exercising this gift a rather dangerous proposition at times.

Yet, the state of our culture is also what makes exercising this gift well so important. Truth is often needed most when it is desired least. It's when lies go unchecked that they can cause the greatest damage, and we see that trend at work even during biblical times.

Our culture is not the first to reject the concept of truth, and it will not be the last. So let's take a look at how God used someone with the spiritual gift of discernment to help transform the lives of his people and, from his example, learn what it might look like for those with this gift to do the same today.

SAMUEL

Samuel demonstrates the spiritual gift of discernment at several points throughout his life. Yet, no single moment reveals this gift in action as well as the general circumstances of his upbringing. When Samuel's mother first dedicated him to the Lord and sent him to be raised by the priest Eli, it was a low point in Israel's history. As the book of Judges describes, "In those days there was no king in Israel. Everyone did what was right in his own eyes" (Judges 21:25). And those who were meant to be the spiritual leaders of God's people often fell into the same sins as everyone else.

Eli's own sons, for example, were called "worthless men" who "did not know the LORD" (1 Samuel 2:12). They would repeatedly take the portion of the sacrifice that belonged to God and assault the women who served at the entrance of the tent of meeting (vv. 13–16, 22). While Eli rebuked their actions, he did nothing to stop them. As such, the role models Samuel had growing up—the men who were supposed to teach him what it meant to serve God—looked nothing like what God intended for his priests.

Yet, despite those circumstances, Samuel "continued to grow both in stature and favor with the LORD and also with man" (v. 26). He was able to discern between the error of those around him and the truth of God. Moreover, he had the courage and faithfulness to act rightly once he understood what that looked like.

For those with the gift of discernment, both are often required in order to fulfill your calling. After all, even Eli understood that what his sons were doing was wrong, but he lacked the necessary fortitude to stop them. However, when Samuel faced a similar situation later in his life, he did what the Lord required.

Toward the end of Samuel's life, he appointed his own sons to be judges over Israel. They, like Eli's sons, were not up to the task and lacked the faithfulness of their father. But when the elders of Israel confronted Samuel with the shortcomings of his sons and asked for a king instead, he discerned the truth behind both the accusations and the people's request (1 Samuel 8:1–9). He was willing to remove his sons from places of authority but warned that a king was not the answer to the Israelite's problems. He saw the way the kings of other nations ruled their people, and the Lord helped him understand that the same would happen to Israel if they proceeded down this path (vv. 10–18). Despite his wise warnings, however, the people persisted in their belief that they needed a king like that of the other nations. When God told Samuel to give them what they wanted, Samuel had the courage to obey.

This pattern of discerning the truth when surrounded by lies was a hallmark of Samuel's life and ministry. He was often the only one who understood God's will, but he still had the courage to act in accordance with it. That pattern is what the spiritual gift of discernment often looks like in a culture that cares more about their own desires than God's truth. As such, Samuel serves as a fitting example for those with the same gifting today.

IF YOU HAVE THE SPIRITUAL GIFT OF DISCERNMENT

If you have the spiritual gift of discernment, know that exercising it well and in accordance with the calling of the Holy Spirit will not be easy. There are times when you will be the only one to see the errors in the thinking or plans of others. Choosing the truth in those moments can be perceived as being a pessimist or naysayer rather than right. At the same time, if you have this gifting, how you relay the truth that you discern can often reinforce that perception unless you do so with the kindness and gentleness that only the Holy Spirit can provide.

Speaking without that fruit of the Spirit is one of the dangers that those with this gifting must guard against. It matters little if you can discern the truth but express that truth in a way that makes it harder for others to accept. For your gift to build up the body of Christ, you must use it in a way that helps others spot the lies and wrong thinking that may, initially, only be known to you.

If you become someone that people don't respect and don't want to believe because your gift leads to a sense of haughtiness or derision that makes others feel foolish, then God cannot do much through you. In such circumstances, your gift will begin to feel more like a curse because you cannot help but see errors that others overlook, with relatively little you can do about the issue. That, in turn, can lead to a second danger.

Because people do not always appreciate when you exercise your gift of discernment by pointing out the lies and errors that they may not recognize, it can be tempting to keep those revelations to yourself. At times, doing so is actually a wise choice and evidence of discernment as well. You don't have to always be the one to point out someone's mistakes. It could be that God wants them to figure it out on their own rather than be told by you. Still, discerning when to speak and when to stay silent can be difficult, and it is tempting, at times, to err on the side of silence.

Just as the body of Christ will not grow and benefit when those with this gifting speak harshly and with insufficient thought as to how their message will be received, God's people also suffer when lies are allowed to perpetuate because those who spot them refuse to do anything about it. If you have the spiritual gift of discernment, then be sure that you also pray for the courage to use it when called upon by the Lord to do so. Be careful not to allow that courage to become overconfidence, though. After all, you are not the source of your spiritual gift, and your discernment should not be trusted fully apart from confirmation from the Lord.

You see, a final danger associated with this spiritual gift is that you become so accustomed to spotting the errors around you that you begin to assume your judgment is always correct. No one is perfect, but the more often you're right when others are wrong, the easier it gets to begin thinking that way about yourself. Utilizing your gift with the humility born of the knowledge that your discernment comes from God rather than yourself is crucial to preventing it from becoming a hindrance to the kingdom rather than a resource.

If you have the gift of discernment, remember to use it always in the power and guidance of the Holy Spirit. It is not a tool to wield as you desire but a gift to be used for the advancement of the kingdom. So temper any temptations toward pride or overconfidence by finding your purpose and motivation in the knowledge that God has given you discernment to help others and has plans to use your gift to that end.

EXHORTATION

*Encouraging, comforting, and challenging
others as they follow Jesus*

The spiritual gift of exhortation is often seen as synonymous with encouragement. While encouraging others is an important element of exhortation, it is not the totality of what the gift is meant to be. At its most basic level, exhortation is about sharing the truth that someone needs to hear in a way that builds them up and draws them closer to the Lord.

That truth is often something that they are doing well or an element of their calling and gifting that, perhaps, they do not fully realize. When that's the case, the gift of exhortation builds them up by encouraging them to continue living in a way that God can bless. At other times, this gift looks more like comforting others when doubts or lies have made it difficult to see the truth of who God made them to be. In such instances, exhortation builds them up by giving them the confidence to go forward with the knowledge that someone else believes in them and their capacities.

There are also moments, however, when that truth may be something that is difficult for the other person to hear. A commonly underutilized or underappreciated aspect of exhorting others to follow Jesus is having the courage to recognize when they are not living appropriately and calling them to something better. Paul demonstrates all three elements of this gift well in his interactions with others.

PAUL

Paul may not be the biblical figure that comes to mind first when one thinks about the gift of exhortation. And, to be sure, there are times when he did not live out this gifting well. He could be brash and unyielding to the degree that he often wore out his welcome in a relatively short period of time. Yet, we also see moments when his uncompromising commitment to the truth helped others see something in themselves, whether good or bad, that proved essential to becoming the people God created them to be. That is what the gift of exhortation looks like in practice.

We see the encouraging part of exhortation in many of Paul's letters to the churches. For example, in his letter to the church in Ephesus, he writes in chapter 1 of how he gives thanks for them "because I have heard of your faith in the Lord Jesus and your love toward all the saints" (Ephesians 1:15). In 1 Thessalonians, he tells them that he offers prayers of thanksgiving to God when he remembers their "work of faith and labor of love and steadfastness of hope in our Lord Jesus Christ" (1 Thessalonians 1:3). And to the Philippians, he expressed his gratitude "because of your partnership in the gospel from the first day until now" (Philippians 1:4–5).

Notice that in each of these instances, Paul is specific and sincere in his encouragement. He doesn't just thank them for being faithful but describes the ways in which they have been and continue to be faithful. These are not empty platitudes or kind words without substance. And, as he later proves in each of these letters, he is not blind to their faults as well. He knows that they are not perfect, but that awareness does not prevent him from recognizing the ways in which they are walking with God and encouraging them specifically in those areas.

This kind of encouragement is not the only way Paul demonstrates the gift of exhortation. In Paul's relationship with Timothy, this gift is seen most often in the way that he comforts the young man by encouraging him to continue on in his faith, reminding him of all that

God has done and will continue to do through him. In 2 Timothy, for example, Paul begins the letter by reminding Timothy of his "sincere faith, a faith that dwelt first in your grandmother Lois and your mother Eunice and now, I am sure, dwells in you as well" (2 Timothy 1:5). He continues by adding "For this reason I remind you to fan into flame the gift of God, which is in you through the laying on of my hands, for God gave us a spirit not of fear but of power and love and self-control" (vv. 6–7). In his previous letter to Timothy, Paul had encouraged the young man to remember the truth that he had been taught and to teach it with confidence, not allowing anyone to "despise you for your youth," but instead setting "an example in speech, in conduct, in love, in faith, in purity" (1 Timothy 4:6–12).

Timothy needed these reminders of his legacy in the faith, his gifting by the Holy Spirit, and his capacity to fulfill his calling from God in order to live as the man God created him to be. Paul saw the truth about Timothy's gifting and abilities even when Timothy didn't and believed it was his role to exhort the young man to live up to his potential in Christ.

If you have the gift of exhortation, then there will be times when you too are called to remind people of the potential they have in the Lord, even when they don't see it themselves. As with the first element of this gift, that kind of comforting encouragement does not mean making stuff up or building their confidence around false ideas regarding their capabilities. But when the Holy Spirit shows you the truth about someone's abilities and calling, do not be afraid to let them know. It could be that you are the one through which God will help that person realize their potential in him.

There are also times, however, when helping someone realize their potential requires holding them to a higher standard than they might hold for themselves. We see Paul demonstrate this ability throughout his letters as well, when he writes to the various churches of the ways that they have fallen away from the truth. This aspect of his gifting is seen most acutely, however, in one of his interactions with Peter.

In Galatians 2, Paul tells the church about a time when Peter was visiting the church at Antioch while he and Barnabas were there. Antioch was one of the first churches where the gospel took root among the Gentiles and, as such, it made many of the Jewish Christians back in Jerusalem a bit wary of fully accepting the Lord's work there. When Peter came, Paul describes how he started off eating with the Gentiles until men associated with James and "the circumcision party" arrived as well. When they got there, Peter, the other Jews, and even Barnabas separated themselves from the Gentile believers and began acting in ways that were "not in step with the truth of the gospel" (Galatians 2:14).

Paul then confronted Peter in front of everyone and, while we are not told how Peter responded, it seems like Paul's exhortation in this moment helped to quell any divisions that may have otherwise arisen in Antioch. It also seems likely that, by that exhorting Peter and the others to recognize their sin and do better, this interaction may have played a role in both Peter and James eventually supporting Paul and Barnabas's position at the Jerusalem Council, where they decided that Gentiles did not need to be circumcised or follow the Jewish law in order to be Christians (Acts 15:1–35). As such, we see God using Paul's willingness to confront sin in the lives of others both in the immediate context of that confrontation and beyond it.

IF YOU HAVE THE SPIRITUAL GIFT OF EXHORTATION

If you have the spiritual gift of exhortation, know that there are many ways in which God may call you to use that gift. At times, your role will be to encourage or comfort others in ways that build them up by pointing out the good things in their lives. When that's the case, do so with confidence, but also with an awareness that they may not always believe what you're saying.

Some people, if not many, are often the last to recognize their own gifting because they are acutely aware of their shortcomings and faults as well. If you have the gift of exhortation, then the Holy Spirit will often give you insights into the abilities and giftings of others that position you to share those truths in a way that can help the other person embrace and believe them.

Just be sure not to get carried away and start offering unwarranted encouragement or comfort. One of the dangers against which you must guard is wanting so badly to exhort others that you begin looking for qualities that aren't there. Some people want gifts that the Holy Spirit has not given them or would prefer a calling other than their own. In those circumstances, telling them what they want to hear rather than what the Lord wants them to hear will tear them down further by encouraging them down a path that leads away from God's will.

At the same time, if you have this gift, then you must also be willing to have potentially uncomfortable conversations with people when the Lord leads you to build them up by holding them accountable. As mentioned previously, this element of exhortation is not always emphasized as much as encouragement and comfort. However, if you have this spiritual gift, then God has also given you the capacity to have these tough conversations in a way that is less likely to lead to division or pain. That can never be guaranteed: you are not responsible for how the other person responds to accountability. But if you have a history of encouraging and supporting them, then you are positioned well to also be able to confront them when the situation calls for it. Moreover, if you have a pattern of speaking the truth when the truth is pleasant, then it makes the truth more believable when it is difficult.

If you have the spiritual gift of exhortation, then the most important way to live it out is by simply speaking the truth as the Holy Spirit reveals it for the purpose of building others up into the people God created them to be. There will be occasions when using your gift is more pleasant than others, but remaining faithful and consistent to follow the Lord's guidance is the key. So go forward with confidence and know that the same Spirit that exhorts others through you will exhort you as well as you seek to use your gift to the glory of God.

KNOWLEDGE

*Understanding and sharing the deep
truths of God's word and will*

The spiritual gift of knowledge is, in many ways, similar to that of wisdom. While Paul writes of both as separate giftings, they often appear together throughout Scripture, with Proverbs especially using the two interchangeably at times (See 1:7, 2:10, 24:5). So how should we understand knowledge and distinguish it from the gift of wisdom?

While both gifts are related to the acquisition and use of God's truth as revealed in his word, the gift of wisdom is focused more on the practical application of that truth while knowledge is centered on its understanding. While those distinctions may seem minor, the differences serve an important role in how each can build up the body of Christ. To that end, wisdom will be discussed in greater depth in chapter 11, and the focus of this chapter will be on understanding and applying the gift of knowledge.

A key part of the role that knowledge plays in building up God's people is the understanding it provides regarding his character and will for our lives. When his people accept that understanding, they can prosper because such knowledge helps them know how to live a life he can bless. When that knowledge is either missing or rejected, though, people suffer because we attempt to relate to God on our own terms instead of his.

Through the prophet Hosea, for example, God warned his people that they "are destroyed for lack of knowledge; because you have rejected knowledge, I reject you from being a priest to me" (Hosea 4:6). Israel's problem at this point in their history was not that they had completely forgotten about God or that they had become an irreligious people. Rather, it was that they had rejected the correct understanding of who God was and how he was to be worshiped. They began to treat him as if he were just like any of the gods worshiped by other nations, resulting in their exile and destruction.

Even in the midst of that exile, though, we can still find examples of those who did not reject that knowledge and prospered as a result. Daniel, for example, offers a helpful reminder of what it looks like when those with the spiritual gift of knowledge use it well.

DANIEL

Daniel was a teenager when he was taken from his homeland and carried off to Babylon. As part of the first wave of exiles from Judah, it is possible that he was either a member of the royal family or the nobility in Jerusalem. Whatever his background may have been, though, upon reaching Babylon he was put into a training program that was intended to raise up the next generation of servants and advisors in King Nebuchadnezzar's court.

Babylon made a point of taking the best and brightest from the lands they conquered and forcing them into service to the king as a way of increasing the kingdom's own status while simultaneously weakening the other nations. The hope was that if future generations came of age in service to Babylon, the nations from which they originated would be more likely to remain their peaceful subjects. While it didn't always work out that way, the idea did help Babylon—and, later, Persia—dominate much of the known world.

But among those taken from their homelands, Daniel stands out as the most successful and capable. The chief reason why is that, throughout his time in Babylon, he demonstrates the kind of understanding that resides at the heart of the spiritual gift of knowledge. Whether it was interpreting dreams (Daniel 2), counseling kings

(5:13–31), or leading the nation's chief advisors (6:1–3), Daniel rose through the ranks of the Babylonian and Persian governments because of his God-given ability to understand and share the deep truths of the Lord's word and will for a given situation.

Moreover, because Daniel used his gift for God's glory rather than his own, others came to know and respect the Lord. After he interpreted Nebuchadnezzar's dream, for example, the king stated "Truly, your God is God of gods and Lord of kings, and a revealer of mysteries, for you have been able to reveal this mystery" (2:47). King Darius declared that Daniel's God was "the living God, enduring forever" and the one who "delivers and rescues" because the Lord saved Daniel from the lion's den after Daniel was unwilling to compromise on his faithfulness to pray only to God (6:26–27). Such prayer and devotion was the source of Daniel's knowledge and gifting throughout the account of his life, and his unwavering devotion to it is what allowed him to rise to a position of authority and respect within the kingdom.

Overall, Daniel's life and example demonstrate the power of this spiritual gift to grant an awareness and understanding of God's truth in a way that helps others know him better.

IF YOU HAVE THE SPIRITUAL GIFT OF KNOWLEDGE

If you have the spiritual gift of knowledge, God can work through you to help others understand and engage with his truth just as he did through Daniel. While your gifting may not elevate you to the point that you have the attention and respect of kings or government officials, he can use your gifting to help others grow in their awareness of the Lord and his will. For that to happen, though, knowledge cannot be an end unto itself.

Many with this gifting have such a love for knowledge and understanding that they seek after information for the sake of simply knowing more. If you have this gift, you may be among them. When that's the case, the temptation can be strong to invest your time and energy in acquiring more information and delving deeper into a subject without thought as to how God might use your learning to benefit others as well.

There's nothing wrong with a love for knowledge, but if the Holy Spirit has given you this gift, then he did so for a purpose that extends beyond your own pleasure and growth. So be sure that you make time to ask him to help you be alert to ways he can use that information or understanding to help others draw closer to him.

Ask him to give you opportunities to assist others in learning how to develop a passion for his word, even if they do not have the gift of knowledge themselves. And ask him to guide your study to focus on areas or topics that will be of use to others rather than just what interests you the most in the moment.

Approaching your gift from the perspective of how God can use it to build up the body of Christ rather than just satisfy your own queries is an important part of being a good steward of your calling. Relatedly, pointing people back to God instead of yourself when they recognize your knowledge is also of great importance.

If you have this gift, then the times you use it well will often lead to others having a high opinion of your intelligence and understanding. But just as Daniel used those opportunities to bring God glory instead of himself, you too must be intentional about directing people to the Lord instead of keeping that attention for yourself.

That said, pointing back to God should not equate to false humility or self-deprecation. It's all right to be proud of the work you've done to acquire the knowledge that the Holy Spirit can use to help others. Just don't forget that, ultimately, your ability to do so is the result of his gifting. Daniel did not shy away from the respect he gained from others or say he wasn't worthy of the acclaim he received. He just made sure that when others praised him, he praised God and helped them understand where he'd gained the knowledge that they appreciated so much.

A key part of why God gave you that ability to understand and share his truth is to help others know him better. If their focus is on you and your intelligence, then they are less likely to engage with him. As such, getting into the habit of pointing others to the Lord when their attention is focused on you will help you use your gift in a way that he can bless.

The spiritual gift of knowledge exists for the purpose of helping others understand God and his will by sharing the truths that he reveals to you. If you have this gift, though, then the passion that you have for his word and the thirst for knowledge that makes learning so enjoyable is a gift as well. So embrace the joy that comes from spending time in study and thank him for giving you the ability to do so productively.

Just also remember not to keep your head so buried in learning that you miss the opportunities he brings your way to use that knowledge to help others. Both aspects of your gift are important, and both bring him honor if done well. So be sure to value both so that your quest for knowledge builds you up *and* those around you to the glory of God.

SHEPHERDING

Helping others grow spiritually

The spiritual gift of shepherding has been interpreted in a variety of ways but often comes back to the basic idea of helping others grow spiritually. The nature of the shepherd's role, however, is frequently misunderstood. Pastors, for example, are often referred to as shepherds of their churches when—depending on the size of the congregation—that is frequently not possible. To be sure, if a pastor is fulfilling his or her calling well, then there should be an element of helping those in their church grow spiritually. However, that growth is likely more the result of the Holy Spirit's application of sermons and lessons than the kind of discipleship that resides at the core of this spiritual gift.

By contrast, those with the spiritual gift of shepherding often thrive best when they can engage with people in a smaller, more personal setting than from the pulpit. It's when they can pour into a person or small group of individuals that they feel the Holy Spirit most at work in and through their lives. As such, Barnabas offers a good example of this gift at work.

BARNABAS

Barnabas demonstrated many gifts over the course of his ministry—for example, he is included in the chapter on giving as well—but shepherding is among his strongest. And though he spent time working alongside Paul to start and develop churches across much of the Roman world, this gift is seen most clearly in his relationship with Paul and, later, John Mark.

As discussed previously, the spiritual gift of shepherding is not done best in large groups. Rather, it thrives in a smaller setting, where the shepherd is free to focus on helping a single person or small group of people grow in their walk with the Lord. For example, the first thing we learn about Paul and Barnabus's relationship comes when Barnabas took it upon himself to bring Paul to the apostles after they were too scared to meet with him (Acts 9:26–30). Because of Barnabas's intervention, Paul was enabled to preach boldly in Jerusalem and was so effective that the Hellenists—Jews from outside of Judea—in the city began plotting to kill him.

Their story together picks back up a couple of chapters later when, after being sent to examine the new church that had started in Antioch, Barnabas left to go find Paul in Tarsus and bring him there to help. Across these two interactions, Barnabas demonstrated that a key element of shepherding is not just helping people grow in their walk with God, but also helping them take advantage of opportunities to use their gifts in accordance with God's will. Barnabas could have simply remained in Antioch and worked with the Christians there to build that church. However, when he saw what God was doing, his first thoughts led him back to Paul and the ways that he could add to what was going on there.

That relationship continued as the two were sent off by the Christians at Antioch to take the gospel to other places. Along the way, they added Barnabas's cousin, John Mark, and Barnabas took it upon himself to shepherd him as well. However, his work with John Mark did not go quite as well as with Paul—at least initially. The young man left Paul and Barnabas at Perga and returned to Jerusalem (Acts 13:13).

Now, that could have been the end of John Mark's story, and perhaps it would have been if not for Barnabas's intervention. However, as Barnabas and Paul were making plans to revisit the churches they'd worked with previously, Barnabas wanted to take John Mark with them. Paul, however, did not because John Mark had left during their previous journey. Barnabas and Paul fought over the issue to the point that they separated, with Paul choosing Silas to continue on with him while Barnabas stayed back to continue his work with John Mark (Acts 15:36–41).

While we don't know much about Barnabas and John Mark's time together, since Acts follows Paul's journey, we do know from the Apostle's letters that he eventually came around on John Mark. And it's safe to assume that a big reason why is the way that Barnabas continued to pour into John Mark and fostered his spiritual gifts over the course of their time together.

Paul eventually saw John Mark as one of his "fellow workers" (Philemon 1:24). Additionally, toward the end of his life, Paul asked Timothy to bring John Mark with him because "he is useful to me for ministry" (2 Timothy 4:11). Tradition also holds that John Mark was the author of the gospel of Mark, likely the first of the gospel accounts to be written. And, given how his first attempts at mission work went, it's difficult to see how any of that would have been possible without the encouragement and shepherding influence of Barnabas.

IF YOU HAVE THE SPIRITUAL GIFT OF SHEPHERDING

If you have the spiritual gift of shepherding, know that there may be days when you wish you didn't. After all, the sense of responsibility that comes with a genuine call from the Lord to care about the lives and well-being of those he brings into your circle of influence can be taxing, to say the least. I'm sure there were moments when even Barnabas looked at Paul or John Mark and wondered what he'd gotten himself into.

At the same time, the joy and fulfillment that comes from seeing a person you're shepherding turn the corner and take that next step in their walk with the Lord is difficult to describe. In many ways, it's similar to the pride a parent feels when watching their child hit those milestones of development that make all the difficult moments along the way worth it. That's not to say you should see those the Lord calls you to shepherd as a child in need of parenting—that approach can breed a sense of bitterness and defensiveness in the other person—but there are some similar aspects to that relationship.

For example, just as a parent needs to approach their child with a clear vision of who they want him or her to become, it is vital that you ask the Lord to give you a clear picture of what he wants to accomplish through you in the other person's life before you start really pouring into them. After all, the goal of shepherding someone in their walk with the Lord should not be to turn them into a miniature version of yourself but rather to help them become more like Christ.

One of the dangers against which you must guard in that relationship is thinking that what worked for you with the Lord will translate directly to the other person's relationship with God. It could be that he has something entirely different in mind for what he wants to accomplish in their life and that your role is more to guide them down that road of discovery than to walk them down the same path you traveled. So try to keep an open mind and be sure to let God lead you as you lead them.

Along the same lines, if you have the spiritual gift of shepherding, one of the more difficult aspects of living out your calling well will be knowing when it's time to let go. Those with this gift often feel a strong sense of responsibility for others. Consequently, allowing others to move on when they've either grown past their need of what you have to offer or, more tragically, because they have decided that they don't want what the Lord has asked you to give, can be challenging. The temptation will be to start holding them back as they start to pull away. However, just as a parent should raise their children with the goal of seeing them leave as well-rounded adults, you too must always remember that the nature of these relationships is meant to be transitory.

That's not to say you'll never see them again or that your friendship and mentorship will necessarily come to an end. However, the goal is to reach a point where they no longer need you as a shepherd. When that point comes, if you want the relationship to persist, then you have to be willing to acknowledge their growth and encourage them to move on to continue developing in other ways.

If doing so is a struggle for you, then perhaps it's a sign that you need to take a step back and reevaluate your motivations for entering into that relationship to start with. Some seek out the chance to be a shepherd because they like the feeling of being in a position of authority and influence over others. That is not the kind of person God can use to help others grow in their walk with him, but it can be easy for your motivations to slip in that direction unless the presence of the Holy Spirit consistently powers your gift.

The sense of responsibility you feel for those around you comes from the Lord and is worth the moments of frustration and fear that often accompany that calling. However, apart from his guidance and influence in your life, those difficult times can begin to feel overwhelming. So if you have the spiritual gift of shepherding, be sure that you start every day and every interaction by acknowledging God as your shepherd before you try to shepherd anyone else. That is how your gift can feel more like a blessing than a burden.

WISDOM

*Relating biblical truth to practical life
with great effectiveness*

The spiritual gift of wisdom is, in many ways, similar to that of knowledge. While Paul writes of both as separate giftings, they often appear together throughout Scripture, with Proverbs especially using the two interchangeably at times (Proverbs 1:7, 2:10, 24:5, etc.). So how should we understand wisdom and distinguish it from the gift of knowledge?

While both gifts are related to the acquisition and use of God's truth as revealed in his word, the gift of wisdom is focused more on the practical application of that truth while knowledge is centered on its understanding. While those distinctions may seem minor, the differences serve an important role in how each can build up the body of Christ. To that end, knowledge was discussed in greater depth in chapter 9, and the focus of this chapter will be on understanding and applying the gift of wisdom.

A key part of the role that wisdom plays in building up God's people is the way that, through those with this gifting, the Lord is able to demonstrate the relevance and application of his truth to our lives. One of the common accusations leveled against Scripture, or Christian morality in general, is that it is outdated and the product of an irrelevant era. The reality is that God's word is timeless and remains the ultimate guide for how we can live a life he can bless.

Those with the gift of wisdom demonstrate the veracity of that assessment every time the Holy Spirit works through them to apply biblical truth to their decisions and situations. Whether that wisdom is meant for your own life or the lives of others, if you have this gift then the Lord has plans for how to use it to build up the body of Christ and bring glory to his kingdom. We see both outcomes of this spiritual gift, as well as an important warning, in the life of Solomon.

SOLOMON

Toward the beginning of his time as King of Israel, Solomon was visited by God in a dream and asked what he wanted from the Lord. His response was marked by humility at the task before him and a recognition of his need for God's guidance if he was to rule well (1 Kings 3:5–9). The Lord was pleased with his answer and said that, in addition to the riches, peace, and long life he did not ask for, God would give him "a wise and discerning mind, so that none like you has been before you and none like you shall arise after you" (v. 12). And Scripture wastes no time demonstrating how Solomon put this gift into practice.

A few verses after the account of this dream, the author of 1 Kings relays the story of two women who came before Solomon claiming to be the mother of the same child (vv. 16–27). Both had babies around the same time, but one of the children passed away during the night. Each woman claimed to be the mother of the living child, and the matter was brought before the king to render judgment.

Solomon responded by asking for a sword, saying that he would cut the living baby in half so that each mother could have part of the child. The judgment was grotesque and in no way keeping with the will of God . . . if he had actually planned to carry it out. Solomon knew, however, that the child's true mother would rather see her son raised by someone else than killed. So when one of the women pleaded for the boy to be spared while the other was fine with his destruction, Solomon knew who the real mother was. As a result, "all Israel heard of the judgment that the king had rendered, and they stood in awe of the king, because they perceived that the wisdom of God was in him to do justice" (v. 28).

Solomon's reputation for wisdom quickly spread beyond the boundaries of Israel as well.

When the queen of Sheba—most likely a kingdom near modern-day Ethiopia—"heard of the fame of Solomon concerning the name of the LORD, she came to test him with hard questions" (1 Kings 10:1). After spending time with him, she came to the conclusion that "The report was true that I heard in my own land of your words and of your wisdom . . . Blessed be the LORD your God, who has delighted in you and set you on the throne of Israel! Because the LORD loved Israel forever, he has made you king" (10:6, 9).

More specific examples of Solomon's wisdom can be found in the book of Proverbs. There, he writes frequently on its importance while also giving numerous examples of relating biblical truth about God and his character to practical life in a manner that offers guidance on how to live in a way the Lord can bless. However, any discussion of Solomon's wisdom would not be complete without acknowledging that he did not always put his gifting to good use in his own life or rule.

Despite his spiritual gift of wisdom and the countless lives he has helped through its use, Solomon eventually reached the point that he failed to relate biblical truth to his own life. By marrying foreign women from lands where the Lord had forbidden his people to have any relations, his heart was led astray and he began to worship other gods (1 Kings 11:1–6). Moreover, by the end of his time as king, he had taxed and worked the people of Israel to such an extent that they began to rebel against his rule (vv. 26–40). Israel would split soon after Solomon's death, when his son Rehoboam followed in his steps and refused to lessen the burden placed on the nation's citizens (12:1–17).

Thus, we are reminded that there is an important difference between having the gift of wisdom and putting it to good use. Solomon knew God's word and his commands regarding worshiping other gods and how to rule justly, but he stopped applying those truths to his own life, even as he preached their necessity to others. While the Lord still redeemed those efforts to an extent, the impact of his sin extended well beyond himself. So, as we think about what it means to have the gift of wisdom and use it as the Holy Spirit intends, let's remember both the good and the bad from Solomon's example.

IF YOU HAVE THE SPIRITUAL GIFT OF WISDOM

The spiritual gift of wisdom is intended to help those with this gifting relate biblical truth to practical life in ways that build up both the individual and the body of Christ. If you have this gift, then understand that both applications play an important role in its proper use. One of the dangers against which you must guard is focusing so much on one of those aspects that you neglect the other.

If, for example, you get into the pattern of applying the Lord's wisdom as it pertains to your own life without giving thought to how it might apply to others, then your personal relationship with the Lord may flourish for a time, but the body of Christ will not be built up. While the Holy Spirit wants to help you understand how to be wise in your own life, if you content yourself solely with that application, a time will come when you are outside of God's will, and your connection to God as the source of your gift's strength will begin to wane.

At the same time, if you begin to make your gift available to others, offering insights into how Scripture applies to their lives and decisions, then you can make a genuine difference in how people walk with the Lord. However, if you become so focused on them that you forget to rely on the Spirit's wisdom in your own life, then you are also more prone to sever that connection to the Lord by failing to live out his truth.

If you are living out your gifting well, it's unlikely that you will wake up one day and simply decide that you no longer want to rely on the Holy Spirit's wisdom. Most likely, if you reach the point that you are no longer applying his truth to your life or to the opportunities he gives you to help others, it will be because you have taken for granted your need to rely on him for that wisdom. That transition into self-reliance is often gradual and becomes easier to fall into the more you use your gifting well.

It can be easy to reach a point where you simply assume that the wisdom and insights you have into God's word will always be there. You can grow so accustomed to knowing how to apply his truth to a given situation that you begin to do it in your own strength instead of his. Over time, you are likely to build up enough basic principles and stored wisdom to speak intelligently and understandably to a variety of situations. Apart from the Holy Spirit's continued guidance, however, it can be easy for divine wisdom to become human wisdom. When that happens, everyone suffers.

A final danger against which you must guard if you have the gift of wisdom is becoming jaded when you are given a relevant and helpful insight from the Lord, but others reject it. People do not always find God's wisdom preferable to their own, and there will be times when the Holy Spirit gives you insights into his will that others don't want to hear. When that happens and the Lord's perspective is proven correct, it can be tempting to either refuse to share his insights the next time or to hold it against the person who rejected it. Neither outcome will build up the body of Christ, though, and going down that path means sinning in a way that weakens your own connection to the Spirit.

If you have the gift of wisdom, remember that you are not the source of the insights and applications that God grants you into his word and will. While your own study, intelligence, and thoughtfulness play a key role in the application of your gift and are essential qualities for the Holy Spirit's work in and through your life, apart from his help, any wisdom you have to offer will be less than what he has to give.

And that's a good thing.

After all, your gift is meant to draw people to the Lord in a way that builds them up beyond what they may gain from any single situation. That outcome happens best when his presence and power are an essential part of the process. So the next time he gives you a chance to use your gift to help others or gain insights into your own life, be sure to remember that he is the true source of that wisdom and give him the glory.

THE PARADIGM GIFTS

While "paradigm" may seem like an odd title—and, admittedly, the alliteration with public and private played a role in its selection—it fits well with this category of spiritual gifts. You see, the spiritual gifts included in this section are those that every Christian is called to practice but that come more naturally to some than others.

As mentioned in the introduction, God does not give us the option to not share the gospel simply because we do not have the gift of evangelism. And the same is true for faith, hospitality, and the rest of these spiritual gifts. Consequently, if your gifting is in this area, know that an important part of your calling will be demonstrating to others what it looks like to be used by God to live out this aspect of a faithful walk with him.

Paradigm gifts include:

- Evangelism: Sharing the gospel effectively and passionately
- Faith: Seeing God's plan and following it with a passion and commitment that inspires others to do the same
- Giving: Investing with unusual sacrifice and joy in God's kingdom
- Hospitality: Using your home and/or resources to help others follow Jesus
- Mercy: Showing God's grace to hurting people with unusual passion
- Serving: Meeting practical needs with unusual sacrifice and joy

It is also possible—if not probable—that you will have giftings in other areas as well. As such, the practical application of these gifts may not look the same for everyone.

For example, there are multiple ways that God may call people with the gift of evangelism to share his good news with others. Some may be more comfortable in one-to-one conversations while the Holy Spirit empowers others to share the gospel in larger group settings. Hospitality could manifest as opening your home to others or having a passion for welcoming those who look lost and out of place at church.

Regardless of how the Holy Spirit uses your particular gifts, though, if they fall into this category, then making sure that you remain open to God using you as an example of how to live out these aspects of the Christian life well is an important part of fulfilling your calling.

As we prepare to look at each of these gifts in greater detail, remember that only God gets the final say regarding the particulars of how your gifts are supposed to be used. Keep an open mind, paying more attention to the general principles that comprise what it means to live out your gifting than to trying to fit your gifts into any particular mold.

And pray that the Holy Spirit will help any truths in these pages that are of particular relevance to your life and calling resonate in a way that helps you grow in your walk with him and your understanding of how he wants your gifts to be used.

EVANGELISM

Sharing the gospel effectively and passionately

The spiritual gift of evangelism is, in many ways, one of the easiest to understand. If you've been a Christian for long, chances are that you have been encouraged to share your faith—or at least be willing to—on multiple occasions. And for good reason. There is no more essential task to the advancement of God's kingdom than sharing his good news with others.

At the same time, that task comes more naturally to some than others. Those with the spiritual gift of evangelism have been gifted by the Holy Spirit to share their faith with a kind of passion and effectiveness that inspires others to do the same.

Or, at least, it should.

As we'll discuss toward the end of this chapter, you are not responsible for the choices of others. That pertains both to how the lost respond to the gospel and how other Christians respond to your example. However, it is also important to remember that the same Spirit who has gifted you to share the good news of Jesus empowers other believers to share that good news as well. As such, if you have the spiritual gift of evangelism, then the body of Christ needs you to show us what that Spirit-led presentation of the gospel looks like so that when we are called to do the same, we'll have a better idea of what all that entails.

For nearly two thousand years, God has been using the example of Philip the evangelist to accomplish that feat.

PHILIP THE EVANGELIST

Two Philips are mentioned in Scripture who were disciples of Jesus. One was part of the original twelve and was from Bethsaida in Galilee. He began as a disciple of

John the Baptist (John 1:43) and eventually introduced Nathanael to Jesus, who also became one of the twelve. We don't know for certain how his story ended, though tradition holds that he may have been martyred somewhere near modern-day Turkey.

While that Philip certainly shared his faith well, it's the other Philip who best exemplifies the spiritual gift of evangelism.

Often called "the evangelist" in church tradition to help differentiate him from the disciple, this Philip was first introduced in Acts 6 as one of the deacons who served alongside Stephen to help care for the Hellenist widows (see the chapter on the spiritual gift of service for more on that story). We see his gifting as an evangelist most clearly, however, in chapter 8.

After Stephen was killed by the religious leaders and the church in Jerusalem scattered, Philip decided to go to Samaria. That's significant because, at this point in the church's history, the thought of sharing the gospel with anyone but the Jews was largely a non-starter. Peter's vision and the conversion of Cornelius in Acts 10 welcomed Gentiles into the fold, but the Samaritans were even more hated than the Gentiles. They were seen as traitors who had abandoned God following the exile to intermarry with foreign people.

What Philip understood, however, was that they still needed the gospel. And in going to Samaria, he was simply following in the footsteps of Jesus, who famously preached to the woman at the well there before spending two days with the people of the city (John 4:7–42). As a result of Jesus' visit, many believed that he was the Christ.

However, we're not told what happened to them after that point. Did they continue in their faith or did news of his death shake their resolve?

Whatever the case may have been, when Philip came to tell them the good news of Christ's resurrection, "the crowds with one accord paid attention to what was being said" and "there was much joy in that city" (Acts 8:6, 8). In so doing, Philip demonstrated the truth of what Jesus had told the disciples in his initial visit: "Lift up your eyes, and see that the fields are white for harvest" (John 4:35).

The harvest in Samaria was not the only one Philip worked to collect, however.

Later on in Acts 8, an angel of the Lord told him to "rise and go toward the south to the road that goes down from Jerusalem to Gaza" (Acts 8:26). He did so and encountered an Ethiopian official reading from the book of Isaiah. Philip ran up to him and asked if he understood what he was reading, to which the man replied, "How can I, unless someone guides me?" (v. 31). Philip then proceeded to do just that, sharing the good news of Jesus, after which the Ethiopian believed and was baptized (vv. 35–38).

These stories offer a clear demonstration of the gift of evangelism at work. In both cases, Philip preached the good news of Jesus with confidence but kept the focus on the gospel rather than himself. Even in Samaria, where his preaching was accompanied by exorcisms and miraculous healings, Scripture is clear that when he spoke the crowds "paid attention to what was being said by Philip" rather than to Philip himself. And the same happened with the Ethiopian, as Philip kept the focus on explaining God's word in a way that led the official to Christ.

Those with the gift of evangelism have a way of sharing the good news of Jesus that points people back to God. While they may be individually persuasive or engaging, when the gift is powered by the Holy Spirit, the Lord remains the focus. Often, they also have the ability to recognize when a field is, as Jesus described, ripe for harvest, coupled with the passion and enthusiasm to work where the Holy Spirit tells them that work will be most effective.

We see both principles at work with Philip, and the results have been encouraging Christians to follow his example for nearly two millennia.

IF YOU HAVE THE SPIRITUAL GIFT OF EVANGELISM

It is important to note, however, that even those with the gift of evangelism will not always succeed in leading people to salvation. While we find amazing stories of success in Scripture, there are likely countless other encounters in which even those with this spiritual gift walked away from an interaction without the other person coming to Christ. After all, God does not force anyone to accept his offer of eternal life.

No matter how well the gospel is presented, there are still those whose hearts will not soften and whose ears will not open to its truth. However, even when that is the case, it does not mean that the evangelist has failed. It could be that your part in that person's story was simply to tend the field and clear out some weeds so that the Holy Spirit can lead someone else to harvest the grain at a later date. That ambiguity of outcomes is why it is vital that those who share the gospel do so primarily out of obedience to God and to bring him glory. Remember Paul's exhortation to the church at Corinth: "I planted, Apollos watered, but God gave the growth" (1 Corinthians 3:6).

If you have the gift of evangelism, one danger you must guard against is getting those priorities out of order. Because you can so often share the gospel effectively and passionately, it can be easier to get discouraged when the other person does not respond in the way that you hoped. As many of the religious leaders in the gospels demonstrate, even Jesus could not win over everyone.

If the Holy Spirit leads you to share your faith with someone, do so first out of obedience to him and second from a desire to see the other person be saved. In so doing, you will position yourself to be better used and empowered by the Holy Spirit while also guarding against the discouragement that can come from seeing someone reject God's truth.

Keeping your focus on obedience to God will also help you guard against a second potential danger: becoming the focal point of your gospel presentation. The gift of evangelism is often—though not always—paired with a personality that thrives on being the center of attention. When surrendered to the Lord, that trait can provide a level of comfort and persuasive force that amplifies the appeal of the gospel. However, when the Holy Spirit is left out or when you share the good news for reasons other than a submission to the Lord's will, it can be easy to become the savior of your own story.

Chances are that you don't have to reflect for very long to think of televangelists or famous pastors who appeared to have thriving ministries only to watch them crumble because their gospel was built around themselves rather than the Lord. Their foundation was weak because God was not the center of it.

When you are the focus of your own story, God becomes secondary and the gospel you share loses much of its power. While any Christian can fall prey to that temptation, it is especially poignant for those with the spiritual gift of evangelism.

So if you have this spiritual gift, remember to use it in obedience to God rather than in accordance with your own desires. Make it a point to surrender it back to the Lord every time you feel led by the Holy Spirit to share his good news. And seek out those who can help keep you accountable to that end.

Every Christian is called to share our faith with those God brings across our path. For those of us without the gift of evangelism, we need your example to know what that looks like and how to rely on the Holy Spirit to guide our efforts. So trust in the Lord and lean on him to show you when and where to use your gift. And know that, when you do, you encourage the rest of us to do the same to the glory of God.

FAITH

*Seeing God's plan and following it with
a passion and commitment that inspires
others to do the same*

Faith is something that every disciple of Christ is encouraged and called to exhibit. The author of Hebrews defines it as "the assurance of things hoped for, the conviction of things not seen" and notes that "without faith it is impossible to please him [God], for whoever would draw near to God must believe that he exists and that he rewards those who seek him" (Hebrews 11:1, 6).

But if all Christians are supposed to have faith, why does Paul include it in his list of spiritual gifts as something given to some but not to others (1 Corinthians 12:9)? How is it that all believers should have faith if only some receive the gift of faith? The answer comes in the difference between the spiritual gift and the general state of belief.

Faith, as Paul describes, is a gift from God (Ephesians 2:8), but the spiritual gift of faith is a separate gifting meant to inspire others to have faith as well. You see, on a basic level, you either have faith in God or you don't. But even if you have placed your faith in Christ and have been saved, it can be difficult to go through every day and approach every decision with a constant level of commitment to him.

The reality is that, for most of us, faith exists on a spectrum. While we may not cross over to the point of unbelief, our confidence tends to vacillate depending on our circumstances and the gravity of the decisions that lay before us. That is why God has equipped those with the spiritual gift of faith to serve as an example to the rest of us on how to maintain our commitment to God and trust his plan. While even those with this gift can have moments where that commitment wavers, in general, they model their faith in a way that inspires others to do the same. We see each of these elements at work in the life of John the Baptist.

JOHN THE BAPTIST

John the Baptist was the cousin of Jesus and was called to prepare the way for Christ's coming from the moment his father, Zechariah, was told about John's birth by an angel of the Lord (Luke 1:17). While we don't know much about his early life beyond that initial prophecy, John grew up to be a man of great faith and conviction. The message God gave him to preach was simple: "Repent, for the kingdom of heaven is at hand" (Matthew 3:2). Yet, despite its simplicity—or, perhaps, because of it—the Lord worked through him to create a movement among the Jews that set the stage for what Jesus would ultimately accomplish.

John's spiritual gift of faith was seen every day that he awoke to preach that message and baptize those who accepted it. The Lord called him to prepare the way for the messiah, and he did just that despite opposition from the religious leaders who were supposed to be the guardians of God's word. His faith inspired others to join him. He soon had a cadre of disciples who worked alongside him to share that same message and share in his ministry.

It is one thing, though, to have faith when the nature of your calling is straightforward and simple. John's gift is seen most clearly, however, when faced with a moment where continuing to have faith meant being open to understanding and following God's will even when it sent him in a different direction.

As Christ's ministry gained traction, many in the crowds who had previously marveled at John—including some of John's disciples—began to follow Jesus instead. When those who remained with John began expressing some doubt and resentment at these developments, John replied, "You yourselves bear me witness, that I said, 'I am not the Christ, but I have been sent before him.' The one who has the bride is the bridegroom. The friend of the bridegroom, who stands and hears him, rejoices greatly at the bridegroom's voice. Therefore this joy of mine is now complete. He must increase, but I must decrease" (John 3:28–30).

That last part—"He must increase, but I must decrease"—is one of the best demonstrations of the spiritual gift of faith in action we have in Scripture. There was nothing wrong with the message John was preaching or the way he approached his ministry. He was following God's plan for his life and doing so faithfully. Yet, to those looking at it from a human perspective, it seemed like his ministry was losing ground and that his effectiveness was diminishing. Being able to have the faith to say, in those circumstances, that his joy is complete is evidence of the Holy Spirit's work in his life.

It's important to note, however, that just because he had the faith to remain committed to God's plan does not mean he never had moments of doubt.

After his preaching and uncompromising obedience to the Lord eventually got him arrested, he sent two of his disciples to go ask Jesus if he really was the Messiah (Luke 7:18–19). Such doubts were understandable given that Jesus mixed in breaking the Sabbath laws (Luke 6:1–11) and eating with tax collectors (Luke 5:29) among his moments of miraculous healing. John still believed that he was the Christ but, faced with his impending death, it makes sense that he wanted to know for sure.

In response, Jesus told the two disciples John sent, "Go and tell John what you have seen and heard: the blind receive their sight, the lame walk, lepers are cleansed, and the deaf hear, the dead are raised up, the poor have good news preached to them. And blessed is the one who is not offended by me" (Luke 7:22–23). After they left, Jesus turned to the crowds and said, "Among those born of women none is greater than John" (v. 28).

Having the spiritual gift of faith does not mean you will never waver in your commitment to the Lord. Nor does it mean that there will not be some moments when it is more difficult to believe than others. Jesus did not question John's faith or criticize him for wanting certainty. Rather, he simply encouraged him to continue on in the faith he had exhibited for so long and, in so doing, encouraged John's disciples to do the same.

John's gifting is what enabled him to remain steadfastly committed to God's plan, even when moments of doubt and change made that difficult. His passion for the Lord spread to those around him and has continued to inspire others to remain faithful across the centuries since.

IF YOU HAVE THE SPIRITUAL GIFT OF FAITH

If you have the spiritual gift of faith, know that there will be times when it is easier to exercise than others, and that's all right. Moments of doubt in your faith should not make you doubt your gift of faith. Rather, it is the way that you exhibit your commitment to God's plan in your life that is most likely to inspire others to do the same. As such, one of the dangers against which you must guard is trying to fake faith during those moments when fully trusting the Lord is difficult.

Part of inspiring others to remain committed to God and his plan is demonstrating that your faith is not contingent on your circumstances. It is easy for anyone to trust the Lord when there is little in their life to make them question doing so. However, when moments of trial come and when God's plan shifts in a direction that requires greater trust in him to follow, remaining reliant on the Holy Spirit to guide and empower your gifting is what teaches others how to navigate similar moments in their own lives.

If you pretend that everything is fine when it's not, it can lead people to think that something is wrong with them when moments of doubt begin to creep into their own walk with the Lord. And if they come to recognize that the faith you display is not genuine, then it can also make them question the times when it was. As such, it is possible that the moments when you demonstrate your spiritual gift of faith most clearly will come as you navigate moments of doubt.

My favorite prayer in the Bible is when the father of an epileptic boy who the disciples could not heal cries out to Jesus for help. Christ responds "All things are possible for one who believes" (Mark 9:23). The father replies, "I believe; help my unbelief!" (v, 24). All of us face times when seeing God's plan and following it with passion and commitment means making that father's prayer your own. If you have the spiritual gift of faith, know that it's all right for even you to have moments like that. Handling them honestly and demonstrating that moments of doubt do not have to shake your commitment to the Lord can inspire others to stand strong in their faith as well.

That said, how you model your faith in the moments where doubt is not an issue is also vital to helping others know what it means to follow God faithfully. If you have the spiritual gift of faith, then recognizing and staying committed to the Lord's plan will come more naturally to you than it will many others. As a result, it is important that you are open and honest about the source of your faith, reminding others that it is a work of the Holy Spirit more than a personal accomplishment.

That's not to downplay how hard it can be to follow God's will or to diminish the work and diligence required to remain faithful. But, if you fail to give glory back to the Lord, then you're limiting what the Holy Spirit can do through you to inspire faith in others. Conversely, if you are as committed to praising God for his gift as you are to following his plan, then when others praise you, they will be directed back to the Lord, who can help them grow strong in their faith as well.

Like the other gifts in this section, living with faith in the Lord and his plans is something all Christians are called and equipped to do. However, because God knows that doing that well will be more difficult for some of us than others, he has given a portion of believers the spiritual gift of faith to help the rest of us know what it looks like to live faithfully. If you are one of those with this spiritual gift, know that he doesn't expect you to live it out perfectly every day. However, in the power of his spirit, you can still be an example to the rest of us. In so doing, you help the body of Christ see and follow God's plans with passion and commitment.

GIVING

*Investing with unusual sacrifice and joy
in God's kingdom*

Giving is a good example of a spiritual gift that some may possess more than others but all Christians are called to do. In the Sermon on the Mount, for example, Jesus focuses on the proper mindset his disciples should have when giving because he assumes they are already going to give (Matthew 6:2).

Most people who have been around the church for very long, though, are well aware of Scripture's teachings on tithing and giving to the needy. We've also probably heard plenty of lessons reminding us that we can't serve God and money (Matthew 6:24) while also being warned that "the love of money is a root of all kinds of evils" (1 Timothy 6:10).

But if all Christians are called to give, what separates those with the spiritual gift of giving from the rest of us?

A helpful model for understanding what the spiritual gift of giving looks like is found in Acts 4 and 5.

BARNABAS, ANANIAS, AND SAPPHIRA

Toward the end of Acts 4, we find a note about how the believers had everything in common, with Barnabas praised in particular because he "sold a field that belonged to him and brought the money and laid it at the apostles' feet" (Acts 4:37). Verses 34 and 35 make it clear that he was not the only person engaging in such giving and that the community as a whole was able to better focus on serving the Lord because of the generosity that characterized their interactions with one another.

It could be tempting to read this passage and conclude that either our churches today should be engaged in the same level of communal living or that such giving was merely meant for that particular period in Christian history. The start of chapter 5, however, provides an important context from which we should understand why God inspired Luke to include those notes about Barnabas and the others.

In this passage, we're told about a man named Ananias and his wife, Sapphira, who also sold a piece of property and donated part of the proceeds to the church. However, instead of praise, both died because they'd each lied (on separate occasions) by stating that they'd donated all of the money they had received for the land.

Their greed led them to try to deceive the Lord and their fellow Christians. Verse 4 is clear that God wasn't mad that they'd kept back part of the proceeds. They were free to keep or give as much as they wanted. The problem was that their hearts were more focused on earning the praise of their fellow believers than on actually serving the Lord. They wanted to be seen in the same light as Barnabas but hadn't given with the same spirit.

And note that we're never told how much each party received for their respective pieces of land. It could very well be that even the portion of the proceeds that Ananias and Sapphira donated amounted to more than what Barnabas gave. Scripture doesn't specify because the price isn't the point. Rather, the point is the faithfulness to give according to the Spirit's leading and for the purpose of serving him rather than ourselves.

IF YOU HAVE THE SPIRITUAL GIFT OF GIVING

Exemplifying the spiritual gift of giving simply means giving in obedience to what the Lord asks of us and doing so with a willingness and joy that inspires others to see God in our sacrifice. There will never be a universal dollar amount attached, and the Lord wanted to make that understanding clear from the very beginning of his church.

Being a Barnabas today doesn't necessarily mean selling property to help provide for the needy (though it can if that's what God asks of you). Rather, it simply means approaching your possessions, time, and finances from the perspective that God is king over all of it, to do with as he sees fit.

For those with the spiritual gift of giving, this approach comes more naturally, even if there are still times when it feels difficult to give. After all, there are times when the Lord pushes all of us to stretch beyond our boundaries of comfort in the service of his will, and even those with the gift of giving may find those moments uncomfortable. That's not necessarily a bad thing.

You must rely on the Holy Spirit's guidance for knowing when and where to give. If you have this gift, one temptation to guard against is simply saying yes when you recognize a need instead of relying on the Lord to let you know when and where to allocate your resources. That doesn't mean waiting for verbal confirmation or a divine sign before you help someone in need, but taking the time to ask God and waiting for him to speak before you act is an important practice to develop. Sometimes the response may be immediate. At other times, it may require some patience on your part. However, learning to recognize his voice in whatever way he speaks to you is a crucial part of our spiritual development, and if you have the gift of giving, this area of your calling may be one way he will help you learn to do just that.

Relying on God's direction for your giving is also important because all believers are called to give, and it is not your responsibility to give to everyone who asks. The community of faith is quite large, and the role God has called and equipped you to play in it is unique. As such, not every good cause requires your financial support and involvement. God will let you know when and where to use your gift of giving if you take the time to ask him. But discerning between his voice and those of everyone else—including your own—requires a level of intimacy and obedience that will only come with practice.

If you have the spiritual gift of giving, praise God for that blessing and rejoice over all those you will be able to inspire and help as a result. But do so with an equal commitment to letting the Holy Spirit be the one who guides and empowers you to use it well.

That is how you can experience the true joy and purpose of giving.

HOSPITALITY

*Using your home and resources to help
others follow Jesus*

Hospitality, at its basic level, is about using the resources at your disposal to make someone feel welcome. In the context of Christianity, the desired end is that the experience of feeling welcome leads a person to encounter the love of God through the love of his people. As such, hospitality is a gift that can be manifested in a variety of ways.

For some, hospitality may look like inviting people into your home. For others, it may be a tendency to be drawn to those who look uncomfortable or out of place. Still others may simply relate to people in a way that puts them at ease.

The gift of hospitality appears in no singular form. That's important to understand because a common misconception is that one has to be outgoing by nature to have this gift. The reality is that God calls and equips a variety of people with this spiritual trait, and the body of Christ must recognize and affirm this gift when we see it in others, in whatever form it may appear.

One of the more recognizable examples in Scripture is Lydia in Acts 16.

LYDIA OF THYATIRA

We don't know much about Lydia's background. Her only mention is in Acts 16, and the details provided there are relatively few because her past is not the point of her story. Rather, she is among the first converts to Christianity (if not the first) in what is now Europe. And God used her hospitality to enable Paul and his companions to win countless others to Christ as well.

If Paul's original plans had come to pass, however, Lydia may have never heard the gospel. You see, Paul, Silas, Timothy, and Luke initially wanted to stay in Asia and continue going east, but the Holy Spirit had other plans and prevented them from doing so (Acts 16:6–7). While waiting for guidance on where to go next, Paul received a vision of a man in Macedonia pleading with him to come preach the gospel there (16:9). So they immediately made preparations and headed west. They eventually stopped in Philippi, which Luke describes as "a leading city of the district of Macedonia and a Roman colony" (16:12).

It appears that there were not enough Jews in Philippi for a synagogue, however, so when the Sabbath came, Paul and the others went down to the riverside to look for any who might be gathering to worship the Lord. They found a group of women, with Lydia the first to respond positively to their message.

Lydia is described as "a seller of purple goods" from Thyatira, a hub of the purple dye trade. Presumably, she'd come to Philippi because it offered a larger market for her wares. She's also described as "a worshiper of God," which could indicate that she was a God-fearing Gentile like Cornelius rather than a Jew (16:14). Either way, once she heard the gospel she became a Christian, and that's what matters most in her story.

After she was baptized, she helped lead the rest of her household to Christ and then invited Paul and the others to stay with her while in Philippi. It's not clear how long they remained in her home. But it's telling that, even after they were eventually imprisoned and forced to leave the city, they made sure to stop by and see her once again before leaving town (16:40). They would return to the city several times across their subsequent travels.

All of that began with Lydia taking it upon herself to make sure that Paul and the others felt welcomed in her city. The Holy Spirit used her and the resources at her disposal to reinforce the validity of the vision Paul received and to affirm that they were correct to take the gospel to the west.

As a result, the church that started in Lydia's home would grow to become one of the healthiest communities of faith of its era and a hub from which the Lord would equip Paul to lead countless others to Christ throughout the region.

And it all started with Lydia simply exercising her gift of hospitality.

IF YOU HAVE THE SPIRITUAL GIFT OF HOSPITALITY

As mentioned, you can be hospitable in many ways. For Lydia, the grandest gesture was opening her home to Paul and his companions, but it likely started by helping them feel welcomed by the river where her group had gathered to pray. In the same way, if you have the gift of hospitality, understand that God may call you to use your gift in a variety of ways. Don't put limits on what that looks like or on the ways in which you will say yes when the Lord prompts you to use your gifting.

And know that the rest of us could probably use your help in knowing how to be hospitable as well.

You see, while God grants some people the spiritual gift of hospitality, every Christian is called to be hospitable to those we meet. That's why, even though hospitality is often a gift practiced more in the background than in front of large numbers, the church needs hospitable Christians to show the rest of us what it looks like and to help all of us become more comfortable with embracing hospitality.

That said, if you have the gift of hospitality, you may have to guard against this temptation: the desire to create an open and inviting space for others while ensuring

God is still welcome as well. There is value in clearing the obstacles that can keep people from encountering the Lord, but compromising the teachings of God's word to make the gospel seem more appealing is too high a price. Many well-meaning churches, for example, have neglected Scripture's teaching that sex is intended only for a husband and wife in an effort to make their congregations seem more welcoming. To be sure, all should be welcome within our communities of faith, but we must not cross the line of affirming sin in the process. The community of faith into which we invite others must remain grounded in Scripture and truth.

So, if you have the gift of hospitality, lean into it and find joy in the opportunities that God brings your way to expand his kingdom by helping others feel at home in it. At the same time, do so with an understanding that there may be some who will never feel fully at home in the kingdom because they are not willing to let go of the sin in their lives. In those instances, your job is to let them know that they are loved and that the doors to our community of faith are always open to them, even if they choose not to walk through them.

At a time when parts of our culture no longer associate the attributes of warmth and welcoming with the Christian faith, hospitality is vital to the health and mission of the church. We need those God has gifted in this area to live out that calling while helping the rest of us know how to do the same.

Lydia may be a footnote in the story of the growing early church, but her hospitality set the table, so to speak, for that growth to occur.

MERCY

*Showing God's grace to hurting people
with unusual passion*

Mercy, whether in the Christian context or in general, is often viewed as synonymous with forgiveness. That's understandable. The two terms can be used interchangeably in a variety of situations. Even Jesus seemed to use the term in this fashion when he said in the Sermon on the Mount, "Blessed are the merciful, for they shall receive mercy" (Matthew 5:7).

While the forgiveness element is a crucial aspect of mercy, there is more to the concept than simply choosing not to punish someone. And that is especially true in the context of mercy's role as a spiritual gift. When Paul spoke of mercy in Romans, he wrote that "the one who does acts of mercy" should do so "with cheerfulness" (12:8). In this context, acts of mercy refer to more than simply pardoning a person for the wrongs they've committed. While forgiveness is part of the concept, it also speaks to acts of compassion that demonstrate the kind of sacrificial worship and renewal of which Paul spoke in the preceding verses (Romans 12:1–2).

Such mercy meets the hurting where they are and draws them to the Lord. It empathizes with their pain but does not define them by it. It invites those mired in their circumstances to look beyond their suffering to recognize that there is still joy and peace to be found in this life. And, most importantly, such mercy helps people encounter the presence and comfort of the Lord at a time when he may feel distant and removed.

In short, those with the spiritual gift of mercy have the God-given ability to embody his grace to those who need it most with a passion and cheerfulness that empowers their response to transcend the empty platitudes that so often fail to penetrate the defenses of the hurting. Few embodied this gift more clearly in the Bible than Ruth.

RUTH

Ruth is a good example of the spiritual gift of mercy for a number of reasons, but the fact that she is seldom the focus of the book that bears her name is perhaps among the most notable.

The first chapter of Ruth begins by introducing Naomi and Elimelech, two Israelites who abandoned the promised land because of a famine and moved with their two sons to Moab. The Moabites had been enemies of God's people since the time of Moses, who had warned the Israelites that they were to be perpetually at war with Moab and demanded that they never allow the Moabites to enter the assembly of the Lord (Deuteronomy 23:3–6).

Shortly after arriving in Moab, Elimelech died. Their sons married Moabite women named Ruth and Orpah. But then the sons died as well, leaving Naomi alone in a foreign land with two foreign daughters-in-law as her only family. For someone who likely grew up hearing stories about how God had saved her people from slavery, led them through the wilderness, and blessed them with a new home, Naomi must have felt abandoned and forsaken to an extent that is difficult for most of us to fully comprehend.

That's where Ruth stepped in.

At first, Naomi tried to send her daughters-in-law away. She succeeded with Orpah, but Ruth refused to leave, vowing that "where you go I will go, and where you lodge I will lodge. Your people shall be my people, and your God my God. Where you die I will die, and there will I be buried. May the Lord do so to me and more also if anything but death parts me from you" (Ruth 1:16–17). As the rest of the story shows, Ruth was true to her word.

After working in the fields to provide for them and following Naomi's advice regarding Boaz (Ruth's future husband), their relationship continued to grow to the point that, by the end of the book, the women of Bethlehem proclaimed to Naomi that her "daughter-in-law who loves you" is worth "more to you than seven sons" (Ruth 4:15).

But it's worth noting that, of all the major characters in this story, Ruth speaks the least. It's not that she was weak, powerless, or never had anything to say. Rather, her mercy was demonstrated best through her presence and dedication to Naomi rather than by her words. When Ruth needed to speak, she did, but her actions gave depth to her commitment.

Ruth showed God's grace to Naomi at a time when Naomi's grief had led her to believe that God had forsaken her (Ruth 1:20–21). And through Ruth, Naomi eventually came to know the Lord again. That's the power that the spiritual gift of mercy can have in a person's life. Being merciful is rarely easy, and exercising it well often necessitates a willingness to share in the pain of others. But for those called and equipped by God to serve him in that capacity, there is a joy and fulfillment that comes from allowing the Lord to extend his heart to the hurting through you.

We see that heart in Ruth, and through her example we gain a better understanding of mercy and the impact it can have in the lives of the hurting.

IF YOU HAVE THE SPIRITUAL GIFT OF MERCY

As mentioned in the introduction, many of the spiritual gifts are meant to be practiced by all Christians, regardless of the degree to which God has specifically equipped you in that area. Mercy is one such gift. Every disciple of Christ is meant to share his heart for the hurting and to look for opportunities to extend his grace to those in need. However, those with the spiritual gift of mercy are equipped to do that to an extent that may not come as naturally to the rest of us.

If you have the spiritual gift of mercy, then one of the ways God can amplify that gift is by helping others know what it means to be merciful because of the mercy they have experienced through you.

Dr. Jim Denison frequently says that God redeems all that he allows. One of God's favorite ways to do that is by using our experiences of pain and loss to equip us to better understand and empathize with others when they experience something similar.

My experiences with cancer, for example, have helped me better relate to others who have suffered from the disease because I know what it's like to live through it. I know the fear and uncertainty that comes from being told you have cancer. I know the anger and questions that can flood your mind and cloud your relationship with God in the aftermath of the diagnosis. And I know the sense of exhaustion that comes not only from the treatments but also from the feeling that your disease is the primary way people see you at a time when it's often the last thing you want to think about.

Generally speaking, mercy is not one of my top spiritual gifts. However, when it comes to relating to people with cancer, I do believe it has become something God has equipped me to do in a way I couldn't before experiencing it myself. If you have the spiritual gift of mercy, then you will often be able to extend that same grace to the hurting without having to experience that specific hurt yourself. In so doing, you will help them better know how to help those going through something similar in the future.

However, if you have this gift, you must guard against a few dangers.

The first is identifying so closely with another's pain that it begins to consume you as well. One of the easiest ways to empathize with others is to validate their hurt. However, it's just as important to remember that God's call is to help them move beyond their pain to a place where they can experience his grace and joy as well. That's why mercy must be more about bringing the Lord's presence rather than just your own into the life of someone in need (Job's friends, for example, illustrate the inadequacy of our presence when God's is required). Otherwise, it can be easy for you to fall victim to their grief rather than being the avenue through which God helps them move beyond it.

The second danger is closely related to the first: when you are naturally prone to empathize with the hurting, it can be exhausting over time. At that point, it's easy to become jaded as a defense mechanism against the emotionally draining state of sharing everyone else's burdens. Some of the most bitter and cynical people you meet could very well have the spiritual gift of mercy, but instead of practicing it under the strength and guidance of the Holy Spirit, they attempted to do it on their own. When that happens, it is all but inevitable that people reach a breaking point at which their gift begins to feel more like a curse. While it is important for every spiritual gift to be powered by God, few carry as great a cost for not doing so as the gift of mercy.

Lastly, it is imperative that those with this gift guard against becoming the focal point of healing for those in need. Those who are hurting, especially if that pain is born of neglect or abuse, often form a strong connection with the people who help them. That connection can escalate to a kind of intimacy that is both misplaced and unhealthy. Countless pastors, for example, have fallen into affairs because they did not guard against that tendency or believed they were strong enough to avoid it.

If you have the spiritual gift of mercy, make sure that whenever you help those in need, you are pointing them back to God rather than yourself. Just as the crowds in Lystra believed Paul and Barnabas to be gods after they performed a miracle (Acts 14:8–18), those in a desperate situation may ascribe the Lord's work to you rather than him unless you explicitly direct them to the true source of their healing and comfort.

Those with the spiritual gift of mercy represent one of the primary ways that the body of Christ can embody the mission of Christ to the world around us. Whether it's helping those who are hurting or teaching others how to do the same, if you have that gift then the Lord can use you to draw others to himself in unique and powerful ways. So guard against the dangers and embrace the blessings while you extend the love and grace of God to those in need.

SERVING

Meeting practical needs with unusual sacrifice and joy

The spiritual gift of service can be difficult to describe because it manifests in a variety of ways. Moreover, every Christian is called to serve those around us, so every Christian is called to exhibit the characteristics of this gift to some extent. Those with the gift of service, however, are naturally inclined to meet the needs of others, and receive a sense of joy and purpose that goes beyond simply helping people.

As such, a key role that those with this spiritual gift play within the kingdom of God is helping the rest of us know what it should look like to serve well. They also inspire the rest of us to serve as a means of bringing glory to the Lord rather than just because the work needs to be done. The attitude and approach of those gifted to meet practical needs, when done in the power of the Holy Spirit, stands out and is easily recognizable by those around them.

While Scripture is filled with individuals serving God and his people well, one of the best examples of someone embodying the spiritual gift of service is Stephen.

STEPHEN

We are first introduced to Stephen in Acts 6, when the community of believers in Jerusalem encountered one of its first moments of potential division. The Hellenists—Jews who came from outside of Judea and were more Greek than Hebrew in culture—did not feel that their widows were being cared for to the same degree as those of the Hebrews. Many of them may have come to Jerusalem for the Passover and stayed following the events of Pentecost when the Holy Spirit worked through Peter and the others to share the gospel in a variety of languages.

Rather than meet these needs themselves, the disciples decided that their time was better spent devoted "to prayer and to the ministry of the word" (Acts 6:4). So they, along with the gathering of Christians in Jerusalem, chose "seven men of good repute, full of the Spirit and of wisdom" to meet those needs (6:3). Stephen is the first one mentioned in that group. The painstaking work these seven men did to ensure that those in need were fed and provided for helped that early community of believers continue to grow and thrive.

It's important to note, however, that this is not the only time or the only context in which Stephen appears. Later on in the same chapter, we find him "doing great wonders and signs among the people" (6:8). The Jews who opposed him "could not withstand the wisdom and the Spirit with which he was speaking (6:10) so they stirred up the crowds against him in order to have him arrested (6:12). He then proceeded to preach the gospel before the high priests with such power and authority that they were enraged and "ground their teeth at him" (7:54). When he spoke of seeing Jesus standing at the right hand of God, they cried out, dragged him from the city, and stoned him to death (7:55–60).

What does all that have to do with the spiritual gift of service?

To be honest, not a lot.

After all, you don't have to perform signs and wonders, preach circles around religious experts, or die for your faith to serve well. But it's equally important to note that you can have the spiritual gift of service and still be equally capable and gifted in other areas also.

Some people may assume that those who serve God by meeting the practical needs of others do so because that is the limit of their abilities. Stephen demonstrates how that's simply not true. If you have the spiritual gift of service, know that using that gift well is a reflection of your devotion to God rather than any limitations in your capacity to work in any other way. Also know that, just as Christians have been looking to Stephen as an example of service for nearly two millennia, your gift is meant to make you an example to others today of what it means to serve the Lord by serving others.

IF YOU HAVE THE SPIRITUAL GIFT OF SERVICE

As mentioned before, all Christians are called to serve God by serving others. Jesus made this basic truth clear when, after washing his disciples' feet, he told them "Truly, truly, I say to you, a servant is not greater than his master, nor is a messenger greater than the one who sent him. If you know these things, blessed are you if you do them" (John 13:16–17). If our Lord saw meeting the practical needs of others as worthy of his time, then surely it is worthy of our time as well.

Yet meeting those needs was not the only thing Jesus did either. In the same way, God calls and equips Christians to minister in his kingdom in a variety of ways and some— like the disciples in Acts 6—will be called to focus their attention and gifts in areas other than service. That's why God has also given the spiritual gift of service to those for whom meeting these needs is a primary responsibility of their work for the kingdom.

As noted in the definition at the start of this chapter, those with this spiritual gift are also likely to find the same kind of joy and purpose in meeting these needs as an evangelist finds in sharing the gospel or a teacher finds in explaining God's word.

At the same time, if you have the spiritual gift of service, there are also some pitfalls against which you must guard.

The first is finding your identity in the work you do rather than in the God for whom you do it. Many of those with this gifting are immensely dedicated to the ways in which they help others. They rightly see their work as an offering to the Lord and of great importance to his kingdom. But if you have this gift, then you must be wary of forgetting that the work is not an end unto itself.

Martha was, perhaps, another biblical figure with the spiritual gift of service, and Jesus had to help her see that there were times when the details and immediate needs of those around her were less important than making time to be with him (Luke 10:38–42). In the same way, you must guard against getting so caught up in the good things you're doing *for* God that you forget to spend time engaging *with* God. He must remain the source of your identity and purpose.

The second pitfall is related to the first: when you are tempted to find your identity in the work you do, it can also breed a sense of resentment toward others if they do not appear to value that work to the extent you believe they should. Because the gift of service is often practiced more in the background than in front of everyone, there are many who may not fully appreciate your efforts. At the same time, there will be those who are tempted to look down on what you do as somehow easier or of lesser importance than their own responsibilities. They are wrong for doing so, but unless you are working for God's approval more than the approval of others, it can be easy to grow angry and jaded. If that happens, then not only will your service suffer, but you will cease to be the kind of example the Lord can use to help others understand what it means to serve well.

Your service may take the form of providing food to the needy, picking up chairs and trash after a church service, or simply checking in to ask if those around you need anything. Regardless of its specific form, know that you are an indispensable part of God's kingdom and an example to the rest of us of what it means to bless God by blessing others. Most importantly, though, know that your work is not the totality of what the Lord can or wants to do through your life.

It could be that the same qualities that help you succeed at serving the practical needs around you have prepared you to exercise your other gifts in unique and powerful ways as well. So embrace those opportunities, however they may come, and work for the glory of God rather than the approval of others. In so doing, you will fulfill your role within the kingdom and become an example to others for how to fulfill their roles as well.

NOW WHAT?

Thank you for taking the time to learn more about your spiritual gifts and the ways in which they can help you serve God best. But now that you have that knowledge, what's next? How can you best put your gifts into practice?

First, reflect on what the Holy Spirit has shown you about your gifts and calling.

Letting God be the one to direct your next steps is crucial to using your gifts well. But don't wait too long to start putting your gifts into practice. While following the Holy Spirit's guidance is essential, it can also be easy to justify stagnation as waiting on the Lord when the reality is that we're just not obeying his call.

It's quite possible that God will lead you to use your gifts in ways that you may not expect, and if you are stuck looking for a specific opportunity or a familiar direction, then you may miss his call. So take time to pray and reflect, but do so with a commitment to act in obedience when the time comes as well.

Second, engage with other believers.

This can be a helpful step in knowing how the Holy Spirit may be calling you to use your gifts. Contacting someone at your church, for example, to see if they have any areas of need where your gifts might be a good fit could be one way that the Lord guides your understanding.

If God has called you to a particular community of faith, then he did so with a clear purpose in mind for how you can serve him there. Maybe you're already serving in that capacity and, if so, that's great. Or perhaps the results of your test and the understanding of your gifts that you've gained through this resource have helped you feel a call to serve in a different capacity.

Whatever the case may be, know that even if the match between your gifts and their needs is not always clear, you can trust that, wherever you serve, God can use you and the abilities you have through the Holy Spirit to bless others and help people know him better.

Third, share what you've learned.

In addition to your church, also share what you've learned with friends and family, encouraging them to invest in understanding their spiritual gifts as well.

Because all of us are called to serve as part of the communal Body of Christ, it is important for every Christian to know what role they are called to play within his kingdom mission. You could be the one whom the Lord uses to help others know the blessing that comes from fulfilling that role well.

However the Lord leads you to use your gifts for his glory, remember that you have been given these abilities for a purpose.

Remember too that you must maintain a strong connection to him, or what he intended to be a gift can begin to feel more like a curse.

So ask him and others to help you spot the warning signs of using your gifts in your strength rather than his, and make sure that every day begins with surrendering back to God the abilities he has given you.

Knowing and using your spiritual gifts in accordance with the Holy Spirit's power and guidance is the best way to experience the kind of joy and purpose that can only come from walking in his will.

You've already taken your first steps down that path.

Will you continue?

ABOUT THE AUTHOR

DR. RYAN DENISON is the Senior Editor for Theology at Denison Forum. He consults on *The Daily Article* and provides writing and research for many of the ministry's productions.

He earned his PhD in church history at BH Carroll Theological Institute after having received his MDiv at Truett Seminary. Ryan has also taught at BH Carroll and Dallas Baptist University. He and his wife, Candice, live in East Texas and have two children.

ABOUT DENISON MINISTRIES

DENISON MINISTRIES is a Christian nonprofit where meaningful content transforms lives. And transformed lives transform the world around them.

Denison Ministries includes four brands: DenisonForum.org, First15.org, ChristianParenting.org, and FoundationsWithJanet.org.